Annie Lang's
202
PAPER
PIECING
Patterns

Shauna Berglund-Immel

LeNae Gerig

Emily Gustafson

Arlene Peterson

About the Paper Piecing & Page Designers:

Shauna Berglund-Immel works for Hot Off The Press as a scrapbook specialist and in-house designer. Shauna and her husband, Dave, live in Oregon with their children, Spencer and Kaelin. Shauna collects children's books and loves sports of all kinds.

LeNae Gerig is an in-house designer, scrapbook specialist and technical editor for Hot Off The Press. She lives in Oregon with her husband, Chris, their daughter, Lauren, and their dog, Bailey. She likes to explore new crafts and search for antiques.

Emily Gustafson is a paper crafter for Hot Off The Press. She grew up in Oregon and is now attending Wheaton College in Illinois as an English major. She enjoys scrapbooking, traveling and music.

Arlene Peterson is the newest member to join Hot Off The Press' design team as a scrapbook specialist. She lives in Oregon with her husband, Craig, their youngest daughter, Missy, and two dogs, Kookie and Nike. She enjoys crafting of every kind.

About the Artist:

Annie Lang is a self-taught artist who works from her home studio in Michigan, relying on her husband and three sons to provide inspiration for her whimsical characters. We're absolutely delighted to share her talents with you.

Production Credits:

- ❣ **President:** Paulette Jarvey
- ❣ **Vice President:** Teresa Nelson
- ❣ **Editor:** Lynda Hill
- ❣ **Project Editor:** Sherry Harbert
- ❣ **Technical Editor:** LeNae Gerig
- ❣ **Graphic Designer:** Joy Schaber
- ❣ **Digital Imagers:** Larry Seith, Victoria Weber
- ❣ **Photographer:** John McNally

Manufacturer Credits:

The publisher and designers would like to thank the following companies for providing materials used in this publication:

- ❣ **Craf-T Products** for decorating chalks
- ❣ **EK Success, Ltd.** for Zig® Writer, Zig® Millennium, Zig® Scroll & Brush pens
- ❣ **Hot Off The Press** for Paper Pizazz™ patterned paper
- ❣ **Marvy® Uchida** for Gel Sparkles, Glitter Gel Excel pens
- ❣ **Pentel of America** for Milky Gel Roller pens
- ❣ **Sakura of America** for Gelly Roll pens

published by:

HOT OFF THE PRESS INC.

©2001 by **HOT OFF THE PRESS** INC.
original artwork ©Annie Lang

Hot Off The Press wants to be kind to the environment. Whenever possible we follow the 3 R's—reduce, reuse and recycle. We use soy and UV inks that greatly reduce the release of volatile organic solvents.

For a color catalog of nearly 800 products, send $2.00 to:

HOT OFF THE PRESS INC.
1250 N.W. Third, Dept. B
Canby, Oregon 97013
phone (503) 266-9102
fax (503) 266-8749
http://www.paperpizazz.com

Annie Lang's 202 PAPER PIECING Patterns

FULL-SIZE PATTERNS READY FOR YOU!

I BELIEVE!

Summer Vacation

HAPPY HOLIDAYS

Table of Contents

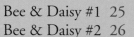

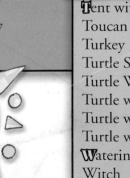

Paper piecing is the art of cutting and gluing papers into shapes. It is a great way to add pizazz to your scrapbook pages, cards and other paper crafts. We at Hot Off The Press know how much you love paper piecing and Annie Lang—so we put them together to create a whimsical way to paper craft your world. Simply collect the basic supplies, follow our step-by-step instructions (below) and you'll be ready to make magic. The only difficult step will be deciding which adorable design to make first. We've provided detailed lists of the Paper Pizazz™ patterned papers used in each piece—but, feel free to coordinate designs and colors that compliment your photos and imagination. There are even dozens of scrapbook album pages with the finished paper piecing pattern shown to inspire you. Happy paper piecing!

Basic Supplies

- Paper Pizazz™ solid, specialty and patterned papers (available in books and by the sheet)
- tracing paper
- transfer paper
- pencil
- straight-edged scissors
- paper glue or adhesive
- ruler
- optional supplies: decorative-edged scissors, assorted craft punches, foam mounting tape, cotton swab or small sponge applicator, stylus, X-acto® knife and cutting surface.

How to Use Paper Piecing Patterns

1 **Choose your pattern.** There are 202 patterns featured in this book for almost any occasion. The finished piece will be the size of the pattern, not the sample image. In most cases, the image is close in size to the actual paper piece pattern.

Ann loves going to Grandma's. As soon as she gets her hug, she runs to smell the flowers.

June, 2001

2 **Choose your papers.** We've provided a list of Paper Pizazz™ papers specifically chosen by our designers for each piece. If the colors or patterns won't blend with the colors in your photograph, choose other papers from our extensive selection. The colors should compliment those in your photo, along with the papers used in your scrapbook page as shown by our designer in the page shown here using paper pieced "Bees with Sign".

3 **Trace the pattern.** Lay a piece of tracing paper over the pattern in this book and use a pencil to go over all the outlines and dotted cutting lines (*there's more about the dotted cutting lines in step 7*). You may also want to trace the interior detail lines from the pattern or draw them freehand after the matting process.

4 **Transfer the pattern.** There are two ways.
- Place the tracing on your patterned paper. Slip transfer paper underneath the tracing paper and go over the traced lines with a pencil or stylus.
- If you're unsure of transferring the pattern directly onto the patterned paper, turn the tracing paper over and place it on the backside of the patterned paper. (Important tip: remember the design will be reversed when using this method.) Slip transfer paper underneath the tracing paper and go over the lines with a pencil or stylus.

5 **Cut out the pattern pieces.** A sharp pair of straight-edged scissors are a must, though there are certain designs where decorative-edged scissors can be used. The scarf trim on the "Child in Snowsuit with Broom" shown here is an example of where pattern-edged scissors can be used. For those small diameter circles and hearts, a paper punch is helpful. We've provided patterns for even the tiniest circles so you don't have to purchase a punch.

6 Mat the pattern pieces. Most of the pattern pieces in this book are matted onto black paper, leaving a very narrow 1/16"-1/8" wide border. There are exceptions, though, especially when using vellum or handling very small pieces. Vellum should never be matted to retain its translucent quality. The secret to making it look matted is using a black pen to outline its shape. You can use the same pen trick for very small pieces or leave them unmatted.

7 Assemble the pieces. Refer to the color image to arrange the pieces as shown. Some of the pieces will be placed on top of others, so be sure they are placed correctly before gluing them together. A few patterns require inserting part of one piece behind another as shown in the color image.

8 Glue the pieces. Once you're pleased with the design, glue the pieces together. You may want to glue the pattern directly onto your scrapbook page or glue the pieces on a separate piece of paper and trim around the finished profile.

9 Add penwork. Now, you can add detail to your design, such as coloring in the eyes, adding a white highlight to a nose, or drawing in crease marks in a robe. If you're unsure of directly applying pen to your pattern, make light markings with a pencil first. Outlining individual pieces with a pen also adds depth to your pattern.

10 Add special highlights and depth. One way to add depth and highlight to your pattern is to use decorating chalks. Using them brings out those rosy cheeks on the face of the "Angel Dangling Three Stars", depth to the "Bunny in Watering Can" and highlights to "Summer Vacation". We've listed the chalk colors with the paper supplies when used by our designers in a pattern piece. Blend it in with a cotton swab or sponge eye shadow applicator.

Tips

• We've provided the Paper Pizazz™ book title in italics for each patterned paper used in every design. When a sheet is available separately, you'll see an asterisk* next to the name of the paper.

• You can enlarge or reduce a pattern simply by using the sizing feature on many photocopiers.

• To get the most out of patterned papers which feature a theme, such as Paper Pizazz™ fall leaves or jelly beans, place your tracing paper in a section that captures the best of the design. Our designers went straight to the center of the Paper Pizazz™ lone star quilt sheet for the pot holder in "Rolling Pin with Hot Pads".

• Add dimension to your patterns with foam mounting tape. Place a small piece behind a nose or fingers that are grabbing onto an item. We've even used plastic-coated wire for the antennae on the "Bee with Heart".

• When working with vellum, handle it gently to avoid creases which appear as permanent white lines. Most adhesives will show through vellum, so use it spearingly and apply it to areas where it is layered behind other paper pieces, as shown with the angel on this page. A glue stick works best.

• Don't be shy about customizing a design to fit your needs! Combining "Sun with Glasses" and "Frolicking Flower Blossoms" will frame an album page nicely. Use our specialized Christmas papers with the angel series for holiday theme pages. Also, look for patterns that match your baby's room when creating the baby series of paper piecing patterns. Let your imagine go—we'll have the papers to match!

Acorns

- patterned Paper Pizazz™: brown plaid* (*Great Outdoors*); fall leaves (by the sheet); gold/brown/rust plaid* (*Jewel Plaids*); handmade brown (*"Handmade" Papers*)
- solid Paper Pizazz™: black (*Solid Jewel Tones*)
- red pen: Sakura Gelly Roll
- black pen: Zig® Writer

cut 1 brown plaid and 1 rust plaid

Angel Dancing on Cloud

- patterned Paper Pizazz™: pink check, pink stripe, yellow/ivory stripe, purple stripe (*Soft Tints*)
- specialty Paper Pizazz™: blue vellum, aqua blue vellum (*Pastel Vellum Papers*)
- solid Paper Pizazz™: dark pink (*Plain Brights*); yellow, light peach (*Solid Muted Colors*); black (*Solid Jewel Tones*)
- pink, purple decorating chalks: Craf-T Products
- white pen: Pentel Milky Gel Roller
- black, red pens: Zig® Millennium

right hand

left hand

lower right dress ruffle

*This paper is also available by the sheet.

Angel Dangling Three Stars

- patterned Paper Pizazz™: yellow/ivory diamonds, yellow/ivory stripes, yellow squiggle lines (*Soft Tints*)
- specialy Paper Pizazz™: yellow vellum (*Pastel Vellum Papers*)
- solid Paper Pizazz™: yellow, light peach (*Solid Muted Colors*); black (*Solid Jewel Tones*)
- red, brown decorating chalks: Craf-T Products
- white pen: Pentel Milky Gel Roller
- black, red pens: Zig® Millennium

cut 3

left foot

right foot

right hand

left hand

back apron ruffle

back apron ruffle

back dress ruffles

yellow/light yellow stripe, yellow dots (*Paper Pizazz™ Soft Tints*); yellow, white (*Paper Pizazz™ Plain Pastels*)

Emma ~ 20 mos.

9

Angel Flying with One Star

- patterned Paper Pizazz™: red tri-dot, green with stars*, forest green pin stripe* (*Dots, Checks, Plaids & Stripes*); crackle* (*Textured Papers*)
- solid Paper Pizazz™: yellow, light peach (*Solid Muted Colors*); black (*Solid Jewel Tones*)
- red, brown decorating chalks: Craf-T Products
- white pen: Pentel Milky Gel Roller
- black, red pens: Zig® Millennium

left hand

right hand

left foot

right sleeve

right foot

left sleeve

wings

back apron ruffles

*This paper is also available by the sheet.

Angel Flying with Three Stars

- patterned Paper Pizazz™: purple smudge (*Bright Great Backgrounds*)
- specialty Paper Pizazz™: lavender vellum (*Pastel Vellum Papers*)
- solid Paper Pizazz™: yellow, light peach (*Solid Muted Colors*); black (*Solid Jewel Tones*)
- red, purple decorating chalks: Craf-T Products
- white pen: Pentel Milky Gel Roller
- black, red pens: Zig® Millennium

sleeve

back dress ruffle

back dress ruffle

Our little Angel

Lauren at 9 months

purple sponged* (*Paper Pizazz™ Pretty Papers*); purple dots (*Paper Pizazz™ Soft Tints*); white (*Paper Pizazz™ Plain Pastels*); saying (*Paper Pizazz™ Punch-Outs™ Sayings #3*)

*This paper is also available by the sheet.

Angel in My Pocket

- patterned Paper Pizazz™: denim* (*Country*); yellow/ivory stripes (*Soft Tints*)
- specialty Paper Pizazz™: pink vellum (*Pastel Vellum Papers*)
- solid Paper Pizazz™: yellow, light peach (*Solid Muted Colors*); pink, ivory (*Plain Pastels*); black (*Solid Jewel Tones*)
- pink decorating chalk: Craf-T Products
- white pen: Pentel Milky Gel Roller
- black, red pens: Zig® Millennium

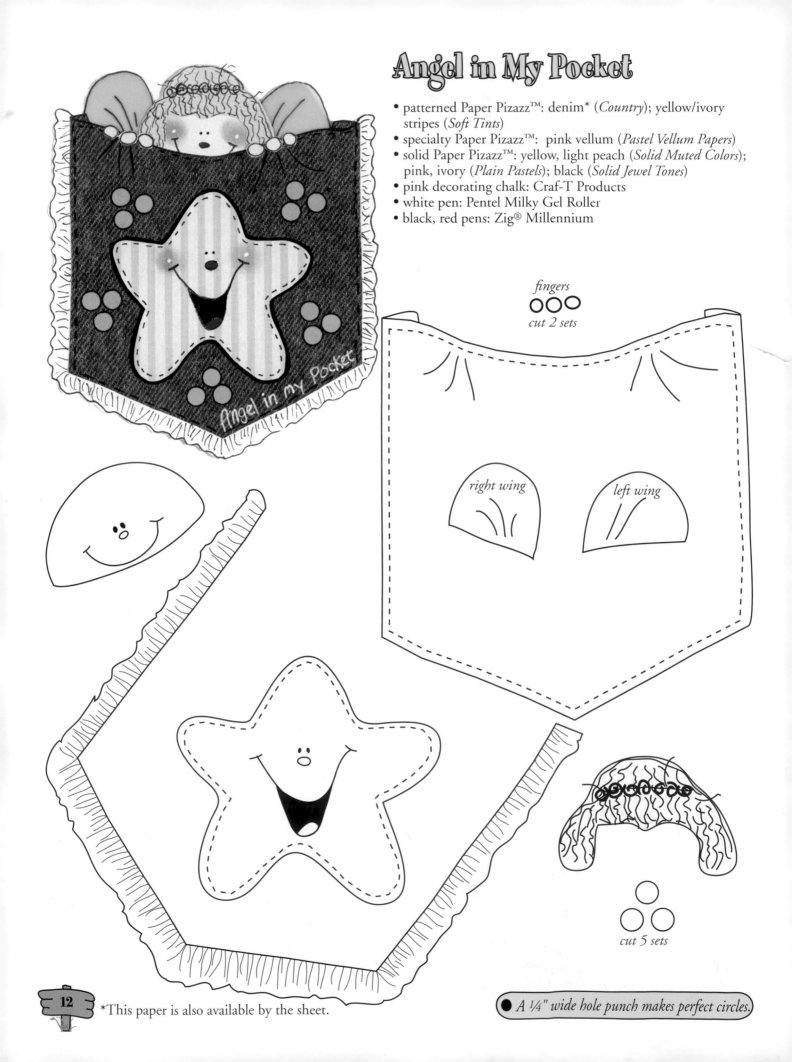

fingers

cut 2 sets

right wing

left wing

cut 5 sets

Angel in my Pocket

*This paper is also available by the sheet.

● *A ¼" wide hole punch makes perfect circles.*

Angel with Large Star

- patterned Paper Pizazz™: red tri-dot, red & white stripe* (*Red & White 12"x12" Coordinating Colors*™)
- specialty Paper Pizazz™: yellow vellum (*Pastel Vellum Papers*)
- solid Paper Pizazz™: yellow, light peach (*Solid Muted Colors*); red (*Red & White 12"x12" Coordinating Colors*™); black (*Solid Jewel Tones*)
- red, brown, purple decorating chalks: Craf-T Products
- white pen: Pentel Milky Gel Roller
- black, red pens: Zig® Millennium

right hand

left hand

left foot

right foot

back dress ruffles

yellow/light yellow stripe (*Paper Pizazz™ 12"x12" Soft Tints*); red & white stripes, red (*Paper Pizazz™ 12"x12" Red & White Coordinating Colors*™); yellow (*Paper Pizazz™ Solid Muted Colors*); black (*Paper Pizazz™ Solid Jewel Tones*)

*This paper is also available by the sheet.

13

Baby Bib

- patterned Paper Pizazz™: green/yellow/pink plaid* (*Pastel Plaids*)
- solid Paper Pizazz™: yellow (*Plain Pastels*); black (*Solid Jewel Tones*)
- black, red pens: Zig® Writer

"Baby" Bottle

- patterned Paper Pizazz™: purple dots, pink gingham, blue gingham, yellow squiggle lines (*Soft Tints*)
- solid Paper Pizazz™: white (*Plain Pastels*); black (*Solid Jewel Tones*)
- red decorating chalk: Craf-T Products
- black, red pens: Zig® Millennium

*This paper is also available by the sheet.

Baby in Blanket

- patterned Paper Pizazz™: pink tri-dots* (*Light Great Backgrounds*); pink gingham (*Soft Tints*)
- solid Paper Pizazz™: peach (*Solid Muted Colors*); black (*Solid Jewel Tones*)
- pink decorating chalk: Craf-T Products
- white pen: Pentel Milky Gel Roller
- black, pink, blue, brown pens: Zig® Millennium

● *A ½" wide heart punch makes perfect shapes.*

Baby in Balloon

- patterned Paper Pizazz™: burlap* (*Country*)
- solid Paper Pizazz™: seafoam, ivory (*Plain Pastels*)
- dark green, green, yellow-green, white, pink, peach decorating chalks: Craf-T Products
- black, red pens: Zig® Writer

*This paper is also available by the sheet.

15

Baby Letters

- patterned Paper Pizazz™: green plaid, green/yellow/pink plaid* (*Pastel Plaids*); tri-dots on light blue*, tri-dots on light pink* (*Baby's First Year*)
- solid Paper Pizazz™: white, yellow (*Plain Pastels*)
- black pen: Zig® Writer

pink bow

bootie ankle band

bootie toe

bootie heel

apron band

blue bow

Baby Rattle

- patterned Paper Pizazz™: yellow swirls, green gingham, blue dots (*Bright Tints*)
- solid Paper Pizazz™: blue (*Plain Pastels*); black (*Solid Jewel Tones*)
- light blue, dark blue, white decorating chalks: Craf-T Products
- pink pen: Pentel Milky Gel Roller
- black pen: Zig® Writer

16

*This paper is also available by the sheet.

Balloon Cluster

- patterned Paper Pizazz™: green gingham (*Soft Tints*)
- specialty Paper Pizazz™: yellow vellum, teal vellum, dark pink vellum (*Pastel Vellum Papers*)
- solid Paper Pizazz™: black (*Solid Jewel Tones*)
- black pen: Sakura Gelly Roll

❧ *Vellum provides a translucent look for the balloons—plus, it works great as tracing paper to capture each balloon face feature!*

Bat & Moon

- patterned Paper Pizazz™: black with white dots*, black/white plaid* (*Black & White Coordinating Colors*™)
- solid Paper Pizazz™: white (*Plain Pastels*); yellow (*Plain Brights*); black (*Solid Jewel Tones*)
- white pen: Pentel Milky Gel Roller
- black pen: Zig® Millennium

right hand

left hand

*This paper is also available by the sheet.

Bear in Wagon

- patterned Paper Pizazz™: pink swirls, blue stripe (*Bright Tints*); crushed suede* (*Black & White Photos*)
- solid Paper Pizazz™: black (*Solid Jewel Tones*)
- white decorating chalk: Craf-T Products
- black pen: Sakura Gelly Roll

right paw

left paw

cut 2

Bear with Bib

- patterned Paper Pizazz™: crushed suede* (*Black & White Photos*); cork board* (*School Days*); blue check* (*Dots, Checks, Plaids & Stripes*)
- solid Paper Pizazz™: peach (*Plain Pastels*); black (*Solid Jewel Tones*)
- white, brown decorating chalks: Craf-T Products
- black pen: Sakura Gelly Roll

18

*This paper is also available by the sheet.

Bear with Eye Patch

- patterned Paper Pizazz™: burlap* (*Country*); pastel pink stripe*, tri-dots on light pink* (*Baby's First Year*)
- solid Paper Pizazz™: dark pink (*Plain Brights*); black (*Solid Jewel Tones*)
- white pen: Pentel Milky Gel Roller
- black pen: Zig® Millennium

inner ears

inner ear cut 2

outer ear cut 2

mouth

tongue

nose

● A ¼" wide hole punch makes perfect circles.

top ribbon end

back ribbon end

Bear with Heart on Shirt

- patterned Paper Pizazz™: handpainted blue, handpainted pink, handpainted brown (*Bj's Handpainted Papers*)
- solid Paper Pizazz™: black (*Solid Jewel Tones*)
- brown, tan, white decorating chalks: Craf-T Products
- black pen: Zig® Writer

paw soles

cut two

sleeves

collar

mouth

*This paper is also available by the sheet.

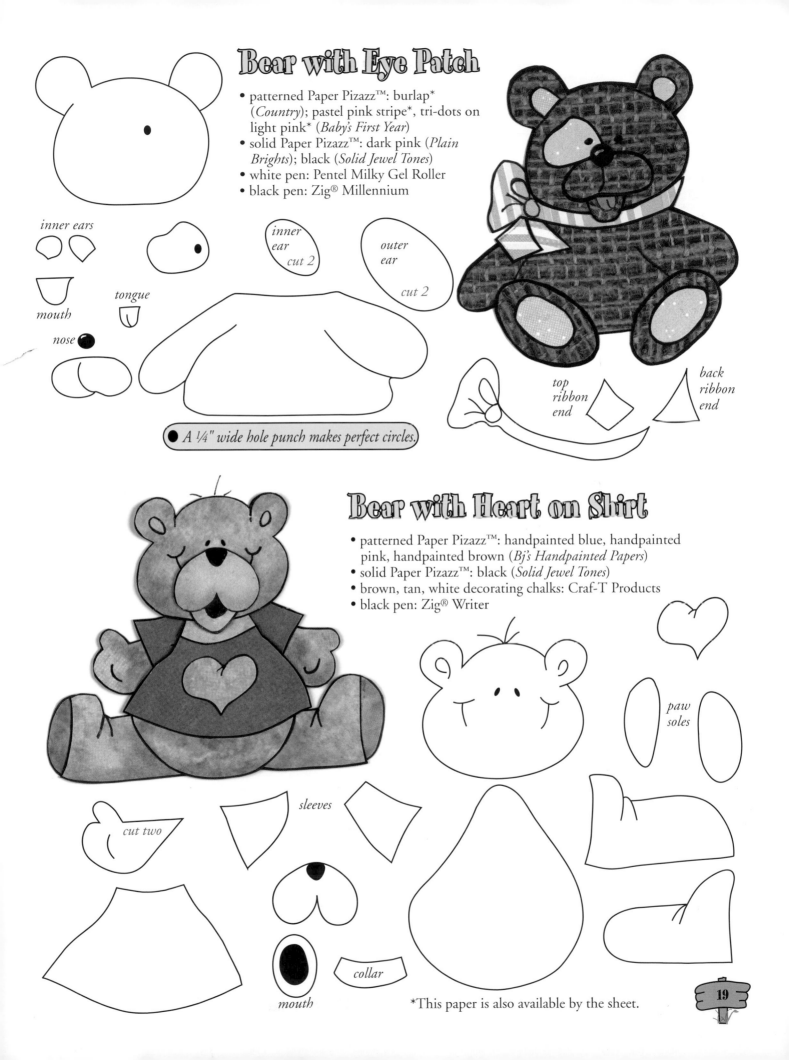

Bear with Hearts

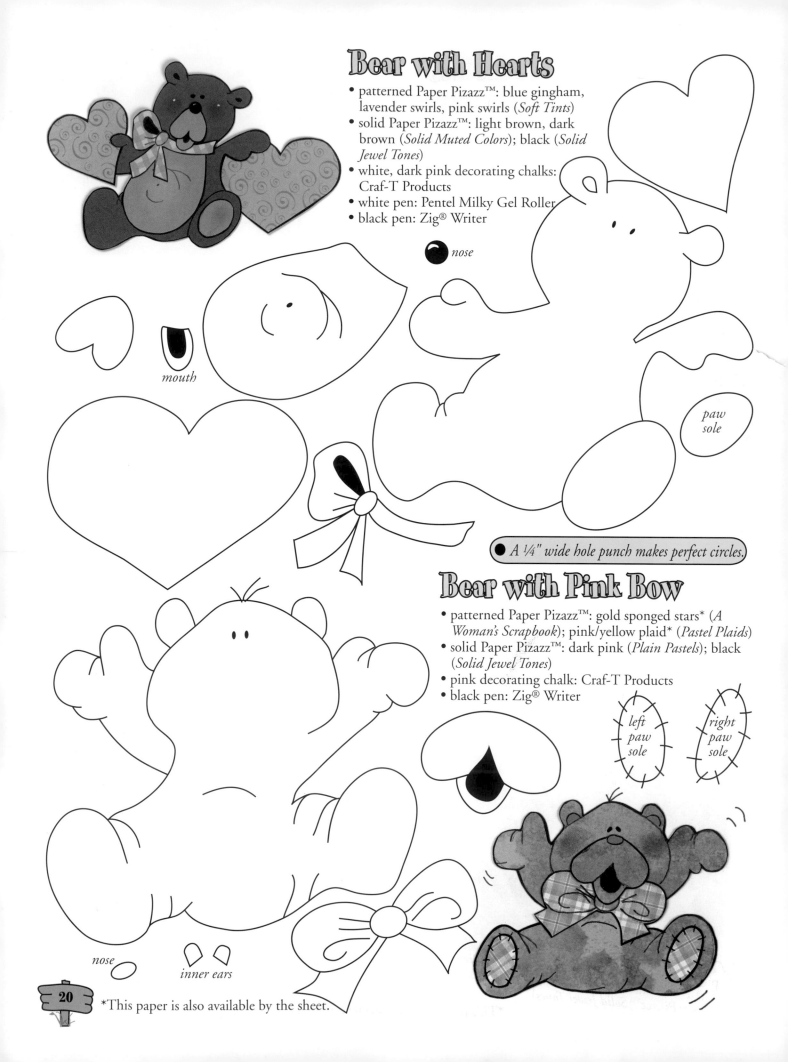

- patterned Paper Pizazz™: blue gingham, lavender swirls, pink swirls (*Soft Tints*)
- solid Paper Pizazz™: light brown, dark brown (*Solid Muted Colors*); black (*Solid Jewel Tones*)
- white, dark pink decorating chalks: Craf-T Products
- white pen: Pentel Milky Gel Roller
- black pen: Zig® Writer

nose

mouth

paw sole

● *A ¼" wide hole punch makes perfect circles.*

Bear with Pink Bow

- patterned Paper Pizazz™: gold sponged stars* (*A Woman's Scrapbook*); pink/yellow plaid* (*Pastel Plaids*)
- solid Paper Pizazz™: dark pink (*Plain Pastels*); black (*Solid Jewel Tones*)
- pink decorating chalk: Craf-T Products
- black pen: Zig® Writer

left paw sole

right paw sole

nose

inner ears

*This paper is also available by the sheet.

Bear with Wagon of Hearts

- patterned Paper Pizazz™: clouds* (*Childhood*); lavender swirls, pink swirls (*Soft Tints*)
- solid Paper Pizazz™: light brown, dark brown (*Solid Muted Tones*); dark pink, blue (*Plain Pastels*); black (*Solid Jewel Tones*)
- dark pink decorating chalk: Craf-T Products
- white pen: Pentel Milky Gel Roller
- black pen: Zig® Millennium

nose

left paw

right back paw

right front paw

cut 5

● *A ¼" wide hole punch makes perfect circles.*

inner wheel

cut 2

GRANDMA LOVES ISABELLE

Hug Me!

cut 2 outer wheel

#

Hug Me!

pink/purple diamonds, pink swirls (*Paper Pizazz™ Soft Tints*); blue (*Paper Pizazz™ Plain Pastels*); black (*Paper Pizazz™ Solid Jewel Tones*)

*This paper is also available by the sheet.

Bedbug with Candle

- patterned Paper Pizazz™: blue diamonds on green tile, dark blue/light blue diamonds (*A Girl's Scrapbook*)
- solid Paper Pizazz™: pink, goldenrod (*Plain Brights*); black (*Solid Jewel Tones*)
- red, orange, yellow, black decorating chalks: Craf-T Products
- white pen: Pentel Milky Gel Roller
- red, green pens: Zig® Writer
- black pen: Sakura Gelly Roll

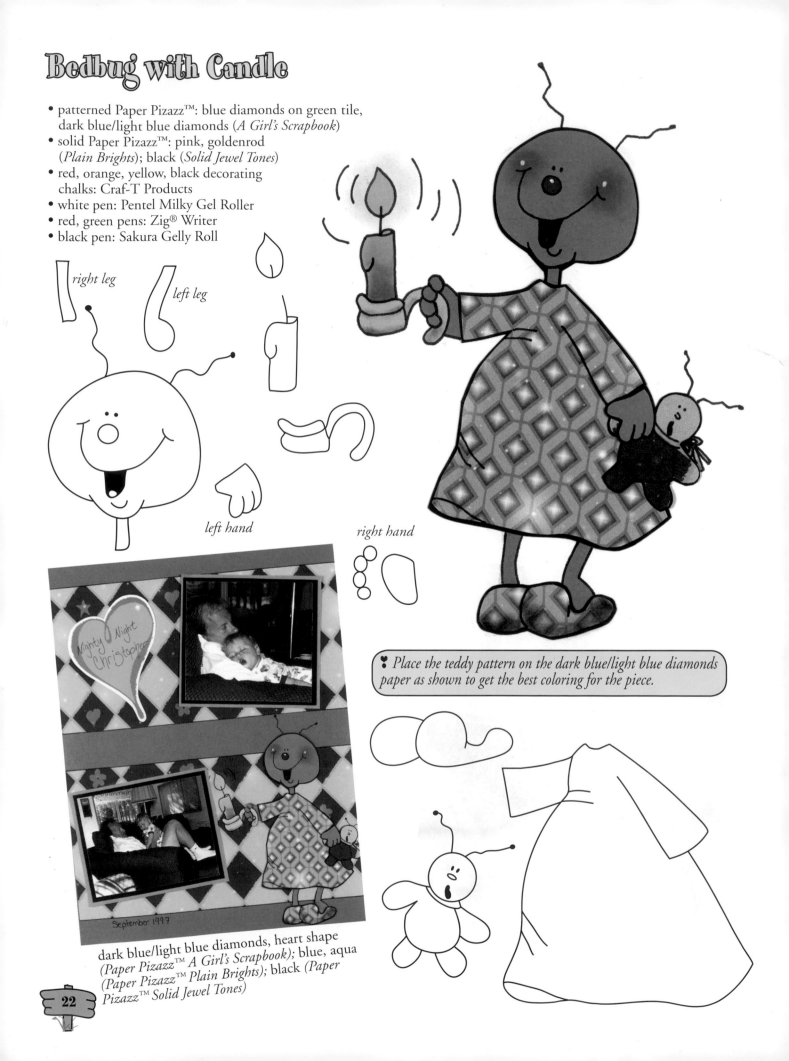

right leg

left leg

left hand

right hand

❣ *Place the teddy pattern on the dark blue/light blue diamonds paper as shown to get the best coloring for the piece.*

Nighty Night Christopher

September 1997

dark blue/light blue diamonds, heart shape (*Paper Pizazz*™ *A Girl's Scrapbook*); blue, aqua (*Paper Pizazz*™ *Plain Brights*); black (*Paper Pizazz*™ *Solid Jewel Tones*)

Bedbug with Teddy

- patterned Paper Pizazz™: yellow check, blue gingham, red swirls (*Bright Tints*)
- solid Paper Pizazz™: blue (*Plain Brights*); black (*Solid Jewel Tones*)
- orange, blue decorating chalks: Craf-T Products
- white, pink pens: Pentel Milky Gel Roller
- black pen: Sakura Gelly Roll

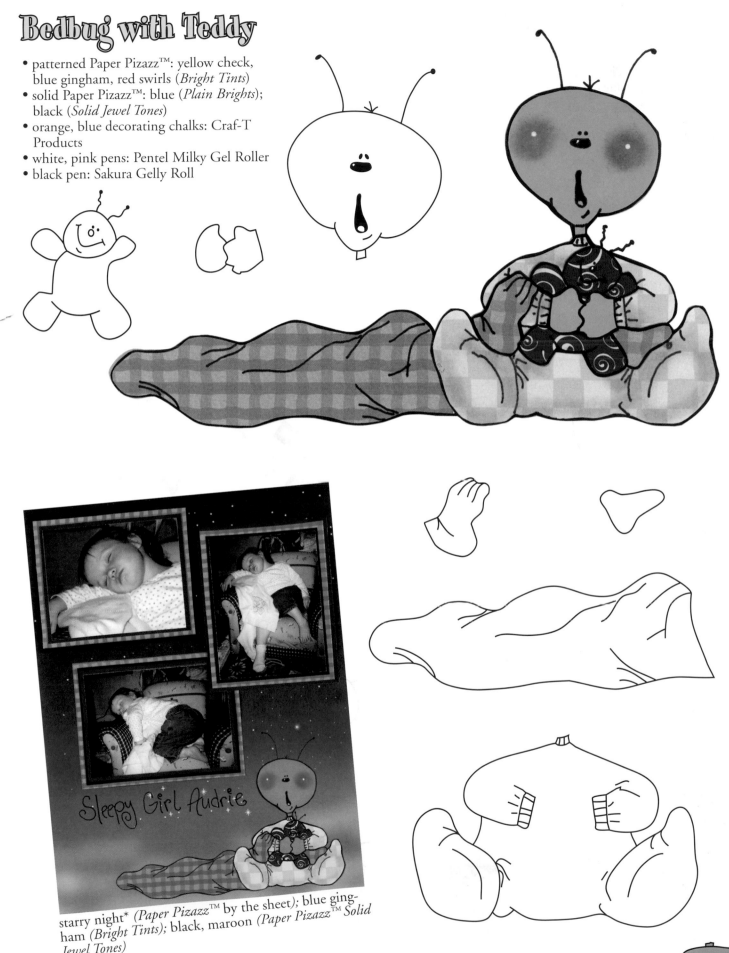

Sleepy Girl Audrie

starry night* *(Paper Pizazz™ by the sheet)*; blue gingham *(Bright Tints)*; black, maroon *(Paper Pizazz™ Solid Jewel Tones)*

*This paper is also available by the sheet.

23

Bedbug Baby

- patterned Paper Pizazz™: purple dot (*A Girl's Scrapbook*)
- solid Paper Pizazz™: peach (*Plain Pastels*); black (*Solid Jewel Tones*)
- peach decorating chalk: Craf-T Products
- purple, lavender pens: Zig® Writer
- white pen: Pentel Milky Gel Roller
- black pen: Sakura Gelly Roll

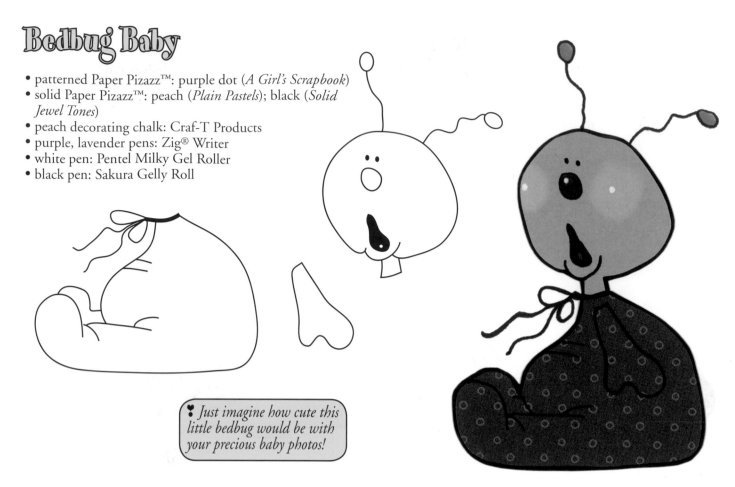

❣ *Just imagine how cute this little bedbug would be with your precious baby photos!*

Bedbug Pointing

- patterned Paper Pizazz™: purple checks (*Bright Tints*)
- solid Paper Pizazz™: yellow (*Plain Brights*); green, black (*Solid Jewel Tones*)
- orange, white decorating chalks: Craf-T Products
- white pen: Pentel Milky Gel Roller
- black pen: Sakura Gelly Roll

left hand

cut 2

right hand

Bee

- patterned Paper Pizazz™: yellow/black stripes, yellow hollow dots (*Yellow & Black Coordinating Colors*™)
- solid Paper Pizazz™: yellow, black (*Yellow & Black Coordinating Colors*™)
- orange-red, yellow-orange decorating chalks: Craf-T Products
- white pen: Pentel Milky Gel Roller
- black, red pens: Zig® Writer

cut 2

Bee & Daisy #1

- patterned Paper Pizazz™: black hollow dots (*Bold & Bright*); yellow gingham, green stripes (*Bright Tints*)
- specialty Paper Pizazz™: blue vellum (*Pastel Vellum Papers*)
- solid Paper Pizazz™: white (*Plain Pastels*); black (*Solid Jewel Tones*)
- pink, blue decorating chalks: Craf-T Products
- white pen: Pentel Milky Gel Roller
- black pen: Sakura Gelly Roll

right wing

left wing

yellow stripes

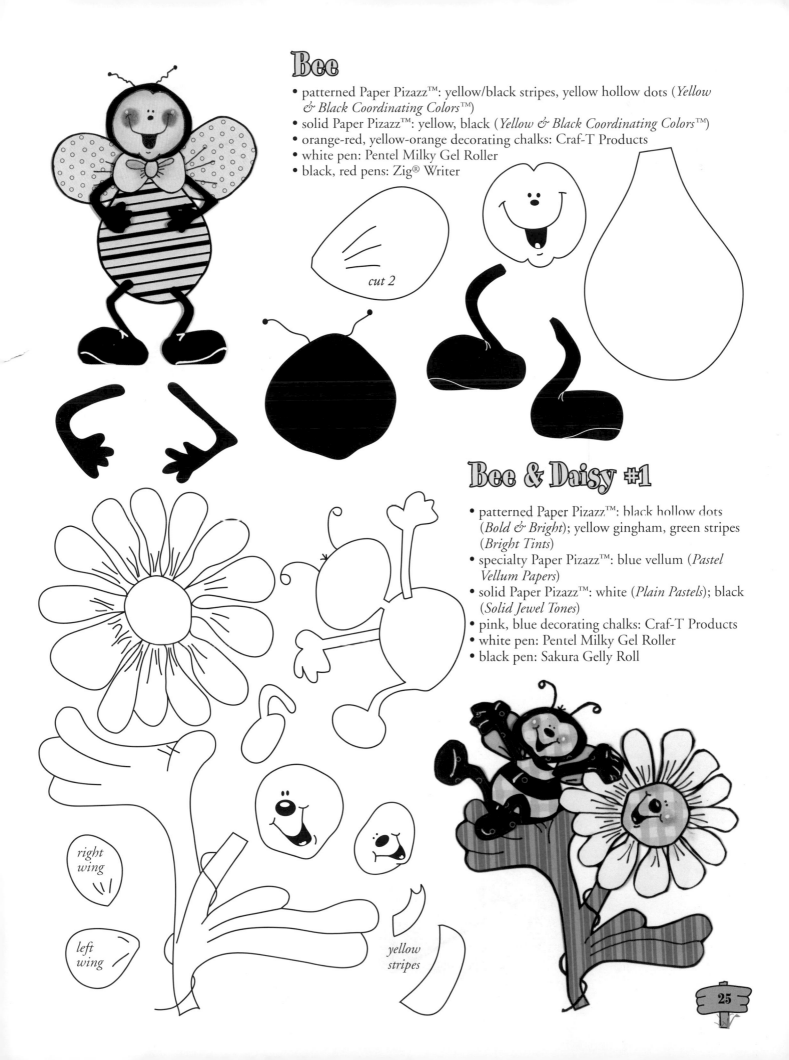

Bee & Daisy #2

- patterned Paper Pizazz™: black hollow dots (*Bold & Bright*); yellow gingham, green stripes (*Bright Tints*)
- specialty Paper Pizazz™: blue vellum (*Pastel Vellum Papers*)
- solid Paper Pizazz™: white (*Plain Pastels*); black (*Solid Jewel Tones*)
- pink, blue decorating chalks: Craf-T Products
- white pen: Pentel Milky Gel Roller
- black pen: Sakura Gelly Roll

yellow stripes

top right stem

left wing

right wing

Bee in Flower Pot

- patterned Paper Pizazz™: black hollow dots (*Bold & Bright*); yellow gingham, red checks (*Bright Tints*)
- solid Paper Pizazz™: black (*Solid Jewel Tones*)
- pink decorating chalk: Craf-T Products
- white pen: Pentel Milky Gel Roller
- red, yellow pens: Zig® Writer
- black pen: Marvy® Uchida Medallion

Flowers For SALE

right fingers

left fingers

Flowers For SALE

Bee in Hive

- patterned Paper Pizazz™: wire & daisies* (*Country*); handmade brown, handmade pale yellow, handmade black, handmade pink, handmade green (*"Handmade" Papers*)
- specialty Paper Pizazz™: blue vellum (*Pastel Vellum Papers*)
- solid Paper Pizazz™: black (*Solid Jewel Tones*)
- orange-red decorating chalk: Craf-T Products
- black pen: Zig® Writer

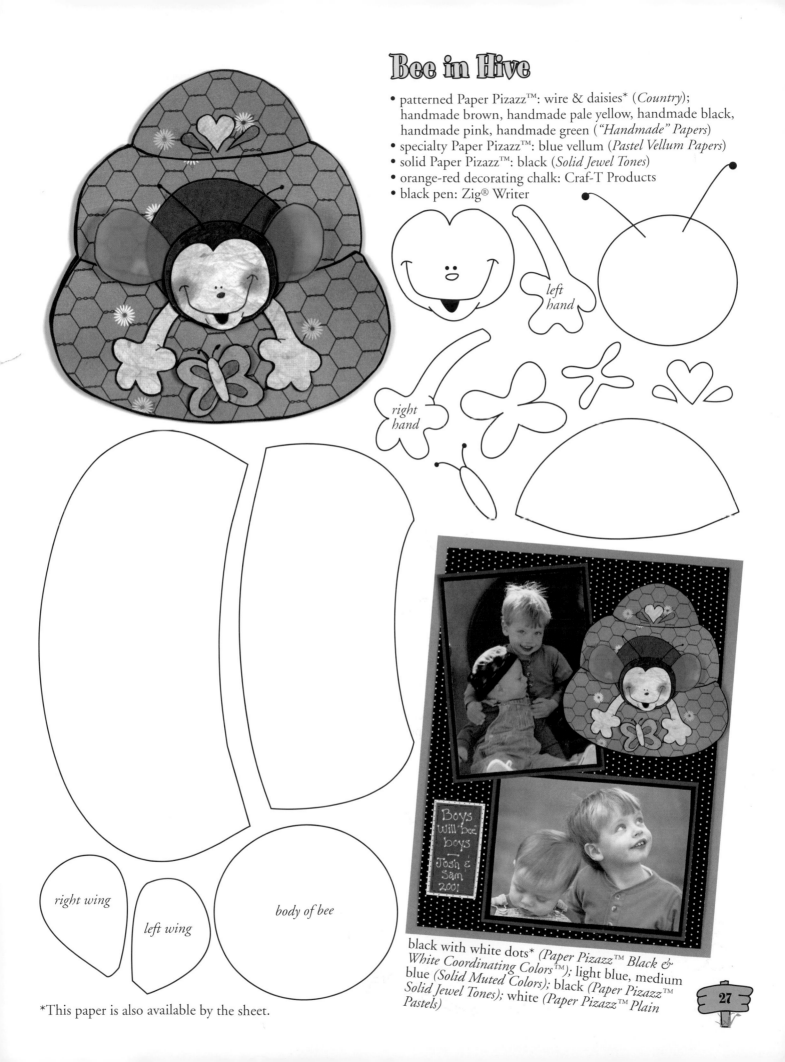

left hand

right hand

right wing

left wing

body of bee

black with white dots* (*Paper Pizazz™ Black & White Coordinating Colors™*); light blue, medium blue (*Solid Muted Colors*); black (*Paper Pizazz™ Solid Jewel Tones*); white (*Paper Pizazz™ Plain Pastels*)

Boys will bee boys — Josh & Sam 2001

*This paper is also available by the sheet.

Bee on Cloud

- patterned Paper Pizazz™: black/yellow dots, red/black checks* (*Bold & Bright*); clouds* (*Vacation*)
- specialty Paper Pizazz™: blue vellum (*Pastel Vellum Papers*)
- solid Paper Pizazz™: yellow (*Plain Pastels*); black (*Solid Jewel Tones*)
- 3½" length of 20-gauge black wire
- yellow-orange, orange-red, gold decorating chalks: Craf-T Products
- white, yellow pens: Pentel Milky Gel Roller
- black, red pens: Zig® Writer

antennae shape

upper yellow stripe

lower yellow stripe

left hand

front wing

back wing

*This paper is also available by the sheet.

Bee Sitting in Jar

- patterned Paper Pizazz™: pink gingham, yellow dots (*Soft Tints*)
- specialty Paper Pizazz™: blue vellum, pink vellum (*Pastel Vellum Papers*); silver* (by the sheet)
- solid Paper Pizazz™: black (*Solid Jewel Tones*)
- white pen: Pentel Milky Gel Roller
- black pen: Zig® Writer

yellow stripes

right wing

right foot

left foot

left wing

*This paper is also available by the sheet.

Bee with Banner

- patterned Paper Pizazz™: yellow gingham, red check (*Bright Tints*); black hollow dots (*Bold & Bright*)
- specialty Paper Pizazz™: blue vellum (*Pastel Vellum Papers*)
- solid Paper Pizazz™: black (*Solid Jewel Tones*)
- pink decorating chalk: Craf-T Products
- white pen: Pentel Milky Gel Roller
- yellow pen: Zig® Writer
- black pen: Sakura Gelly Roll

righthand fingers

arms

left hand

right foot

left wing

right wing

left foot

I'm just a 'lil BUSY BEE!

yellow stripes

♥ *Use this banner to write other messages, such as "Congratulations" or "Happy Birthday!"*

Bee with Bonnet

- patterned Paper Pizazz™: yellow/ivory stripes, green gingham (*Soft Tints*)
- specialty Paper Pizazz™: yellow vellum (*Pastel Vellum Papers*)
- solid Paper Pizazz™: white, ivory (*Plain Pastels*); black (*Solid Jewel Tones*)
- pink, yellow-orange decorating chalks: Craf-T Products
- white pen: Pentel Milky Gel Roller
- black, orange pens: Zig® Writer

left hand

right hand

left foot

cut ↑

right foot

bonnet top

Bee with Butterfly

- patterned Paper Pizazz™: blue swirls, pink swirls, pink gingham, yellow dots (*Bright Tints*)
- solid Paper Pizazz™: ivory (*Plain Pastels*); black (*Solid Jewel Tones*)
- yellow, yellow-orange, orange-red decorating chalks: Craf-T Products
- white pen: Pentel Milky Gel Roller
- black, red pens: Zig® Writer

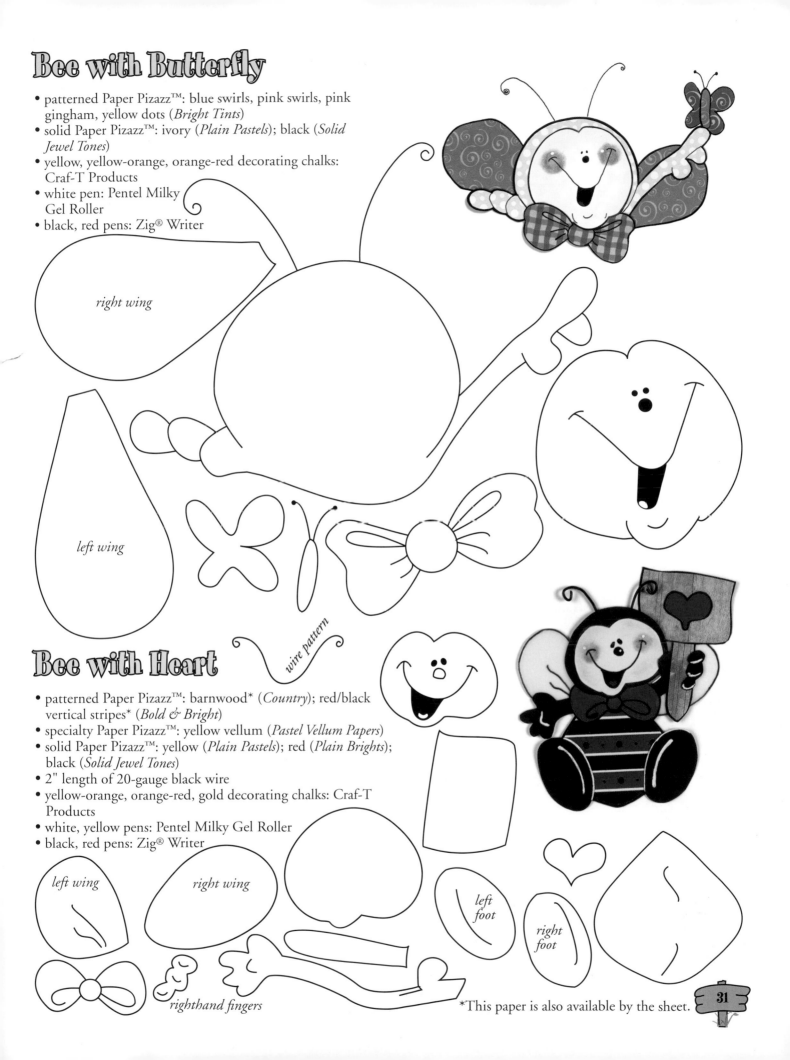

right wing

left wing

wire pattern

Bee with Heart

- patterned Paper Pizazz™: barnwood* (*Country*); red/black vertical stripes* (*Bold & Bright*)
- specialty Paper Pizazz™: yellow vellum (*Pastel Vellum Papers*)
- solid Paper Pizazz™: yellow (*Plain Pastels*); red (*Plain Brights*); black (*Solid Jewel Tones*)
- 2" length of 20-gauge black wire
- yellow-orange, orange-red, gold decorating chalks: Craf-T Products
- white, yellow pens: Pentel Milky Gel Roller
- black, red pens: Zig® Writer

left wing

right wing

left foot

right foot

righthand fingers

*This paper is also available by the sheet.

Bee with Flower

- patterned Paper Pizazz™: black with white dots* (*Heritage Papers*)
- specialty Paper Pizazz™: blue vellum (*Pastel Vellum Papers*)
- solid Paper Pizazz™: goldenrod, red, green (*Plain Brights*); black (*Solid Jewel Tones*)
- gold, orange, orange-red decorating chalks: Craf-T Products
- white pen: Pentel Milky Gel Roller
- black, red, orange pens: Zig® Writer

right hand

back wing

bow knot

front wing

left hand

left foot

right foot

black & white checks (*Paper Pizazz™ Black & White Coordinating Colors™*); black (*Paper Pizazz™ Solid Jewel Tones*); white (*Plain Pastels*)

*This paper is also available by the sheet.

Bee with Candy Cane

- patterned Paper Pizazz™: red with hollow dots*, black hollow dots (*Bold & Bright*); lace netting (by the sheet); red & white stripes*, Christmas candy* (*Ho, Ho, Ho!!!*)
- specialty Paper Pizazz™: blue vellum (*Pastel Vellum Papers*)
- solid Paper Pizazz™: yellow (*Plain Brights*); black (*Solid Jewel Tones*)
- pink decorating chalk: Craf-T Products
- white pen: Pentel Milky Gel Roller
- black pen: Sakura Gelly Roll

left wing

right wing

left fingers

right fingers

yellow stripes

arms

Bee with Holly

- patterned Paper Pizazz™: white dots on green (*Red & Green Coordinating Colors™*); red hollow dots, black hollow dots (*Bold & Bright*); lace netting (by the sheet)
- specialty Paper Pizazz™: blue vellum (*Pastel Vellum Papers*)
- solid Paper Pizazz™: yellow (*Plain Brights*); black (*Solid Jewel Tones*)
- pink decorating chalk: Craf-T Products
- white pen: Pentel Milky Gel Roller
- black pen: Sakura Gelly Roll

fingers

yellow stripes

left arm

left wing

right wing

*This paper is also available by the sheet.

Bee with Merry Christmas

- patterned Paper Pizazz™: red & white stripes*, Christmas plaid* (*Ho, Ho, Ho!!!*); black hollow dots (*Bold & Bright*); white moiré (by the sheet)
- solid Paper Pizazz™: blue vellum (*Pastel Vellum Papers*)
- solid Paper Pizazz™: yellow (*Plain Brights*); tan, slate blue (*Solid Muted Tones*); black, green (*Solid Jewel Tones*)
- orange decorating chalk: Craf-T Products
- white pen: Pentel Milky Gel Roller
- red pen: Zig® Writer
- black pens: Sakura Gelly Roll, Marvy® Uchida Medallion (.05mm)

right wing

right foot

left foot

right hand

left hand

yellow stripes

LET US BEE MERRY

*This paper is also available by the sheet.

34

Bees with Sign

- patterned Paper Pizazz™: green stripes, yellow gingham (*Bright Tints*); black hollow dots (*Bold & Bright*); barnwood* (*Country*)
- specialty Paper Pizazz™: blue vellum (*Pastel Vellum Papers*)
- solid Paper Pizazz™: white (*Plain Pastels*); black (*Solid Jewel Tones*)
- pink decorating chalk: Craf-T Products
- white pen: Pentel Milky Gel Roller
- black, pink pens: Sakura Gelly Roll

sitting bee

fingers

yellow stripes

left foot

right foot

left hand

left wing

right wing

flower and stem

hanging bee parts

yellow stripe

fingers

right wing

left foot

right foot

bee bottom

left wing

June, 2001

Ann loves going to Grandma's. As soon as she gets her hug, she runs to smell the flowers.

yellow dot, green diamonds (*Paper Pizazz™ Bright Tints*); black (*Paper Pizazz™ Solid Jewel Tones*)

*This paper is also available by the sheet.

35

Bird and Cage

- patterned Paper Pizazz™: blue confetti from "Dog with Present" page, yellow check from "Scrapbook" page (*Annie Lang's Heartwarming Papers*)
- specialty Paper Pizazz™: silver* (by the sheet)
- solid Paper Pizazz™: black (*Solid Jewel Tones*)
- black pen: Sakura Gelly Roll

right hand

right claws

left claws

cage top bar

beak

Birthday Boy

- patterned Paper Pizazz™: yellow gingham, yellow swirls on red, blue swirls, blue stripes, yellow swirls (*Bright Tints*); denim*, barnwood* (*Country*); baseballs (by the sheet)
- solid Paper Pizazz™: brown (*Solid Muted Tones*); black (*Solid Jewel Tones*)
- white pen: Pentel Milky Gel Roller
- black pen: Zig® Writer

blue confetti piece

denim bill

yellow section

red section

yellow confetti pieces

red confetti pieces

baseball cap pieces

denim

*This paper is also available by the sheet.

Birthday Girl

- patterned Paper Pizazz™: purple brush-strokes, purple/pink swirls, purple/pink blend (*Great Backgrounds*)
- solid Paper Pizazz™: white (*Plain Pastels*); yellow (*Solid Muted Colors*); black (*Solid Jewel Tones*)
- purple, white decorating chalks: Craf-T Products
- black, orange pens: Zig® Writer

Bookworm with "A"

- patterned Paper Pizazz™: green tri-dot (*Green & White Coordinating Colors*™)
- specialty Paper Pizazz™: blue vellum (*Pastel Vellum Papers*)
- solid Paper Pizazz™: blue, red (*Plain Brights*); black (*Solid Jewel Tones*)
- yellow, pink decorating chalks: Craf-T Products
- black pen: Zig® Millennium

Bookworm with Book

- patterned Paper Pizazz™: green tri-dots (*Green & White Coordinating Colors™*)
- specialty Paper Pizazz™: blue vellum (*Pastel Vellum Papers*)
- solid Paper Pizazz™: red, blue (*Plain Brights*); white (*Plain Pastels*); black (*Solid Jewel Tones*)
- black pen: Zig® Millennium

green check (*Paper Pizazz™ Dots, Checks, Plaids & Stripes*); green leaves on white, white, green (*Paper Pizazz™ 12"x12" Green & White Coordinaing Colors™*); saying (*Paper Pizazz™ Punch-Outs™ Sayings #3*)

*This paper is also available by the sheet.

Bookworm with "B"

- patterned Paper Pizazz™: green dots (*Bright Tints*)
- specialty Paper Pizazz™: blue vellum (*Pastel Vellum Papers*)
- solid Paper Pizazz™: yellow, red (*Plain Brights*); black (*Solid Jewel Tones*)
- red decorating chalk: Craf-T Products
- black pen: Zig® Millennium

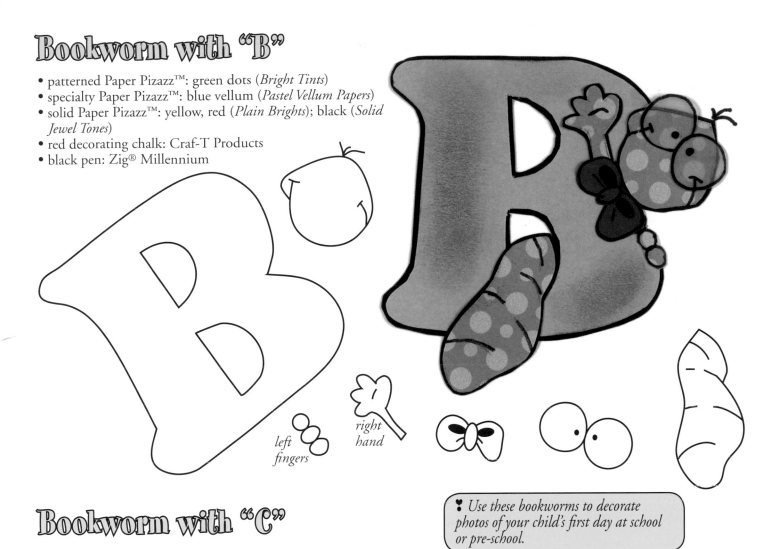

left fingers

right hand

❣ *Use these bookworms to decorate photos of your child's first day at school or pre-school.*

Bookworm with "C"

- patterned Paper Pizazz™: green dots (*Bright Tints*)
- specialty Paper Pizazz™: blue vellum (*Pastel Vellum Papers*)
- solid Paper Pizazz™: red, blue (*Plain Brights*); black (*Solid Jewel Tones*)
- yellow, brown decorating chalks: Craf-T Products
- black pen: Zig® Millennium

Bookworm with Chalkboard

- patterned Paper Pizazz™: green dots (*Bright Tints*); barnwood* (*Country*)
- specialty Paper Pizazz™: blue vellum (*Pastel Vellum Papers*)
- solid Paper Pizazz™: red (*Plain Brights*); black (*Solid Jewel Tones*)
- white pen: Pentel Milky Gel Roller
- black pen: Zig® Millennium

right hand

left hand

Bookworm with Globe

- patterned Paper Pizazz™: green tri-dot (*Green & White Coordinating Colors™*); aqua satin (*Bright Great Backgrounds*)
- specialty Paper Pizazz™: blue vellum (*Pastel Vellum Papers*)
- solid Paper Pizazz™: lime green (*Plain Brights*); black (*Solid Jewel Tones*)
- black pen: Zig® Millennium

right hand

left hand

*This paper is also available by the sheet.

Bookworm with Lunchpail

- patterned Paper Pizazz™: green dots, blue gingham (*Bright Tints*)
- specialty Paper Pizazz™: blue vellum (*Pastel Vellum Papers*)
- solid Paper Pizazz™: red, yellow (*Plain Brights*); black (*Solid Jewel Tones*)
- black pen: Zig® Millennium

lunchpail clasp

Bookworm with Pencil

- patterned Paper Pizazz™: green tri-dot (*Green & White Coordinating Colors™*); yellow/ivory stripes (*Soft Tints*)
- specialty Paper Pizazz™: blue vellum (*Pastel Vellum Papers*)
- solid Paper Pizazz™: pink, ivory (*Plain Pastels*); gray, black (*Solid Jewel Tones*)
- black pen: Zig® Millennium

right hand

left hand

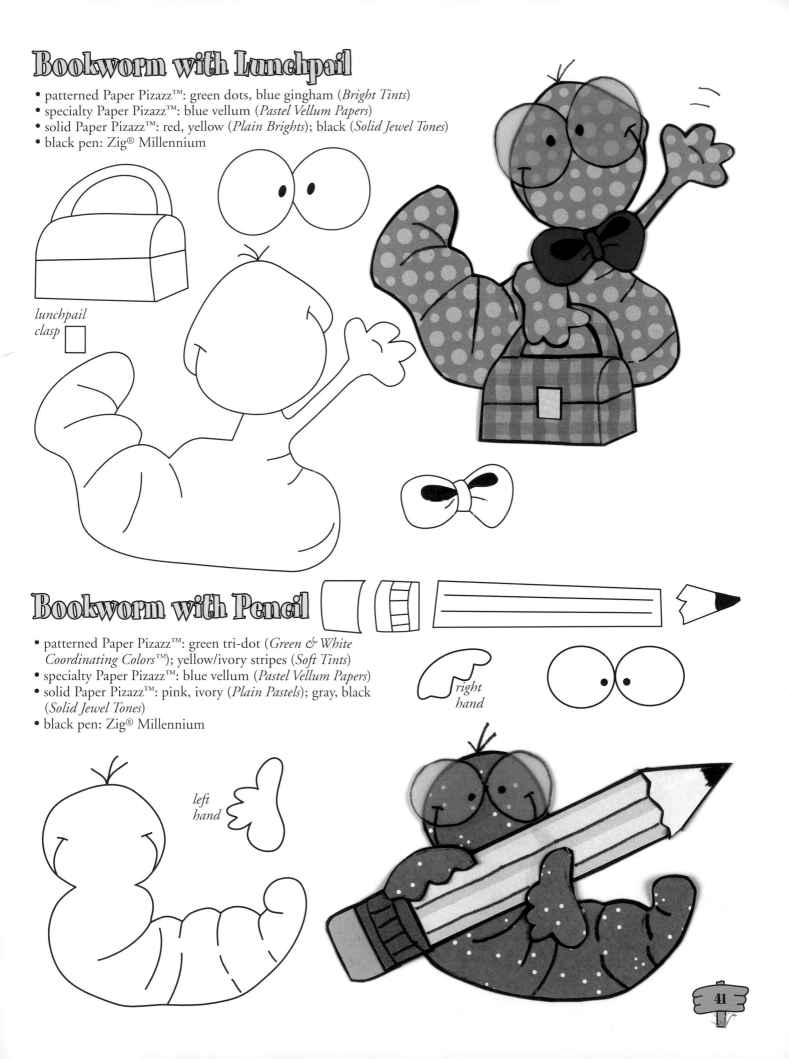

41

Bookworm with Star

- patterned Paper Pizazz™: green tri-dot (*Green & White Coordinating Colors*™); yellow check (*Bright Tints*)
- specialty Paper Pizazz™: blue vellum (*Pastel Vellum Papers*)
- solid Paper Pizazz™: red (*Plain Brights*); black (*Solid Jewel Tones*)
- orange decorating chalk: Craf-T Products
- black pen: Zig® Millennium

right hand

left hand

Bookworms with Apple

- patterned Paper Pizazz™: green tri-dot (*Green & White Coordinating Colors*™)
- specialty Paper Pizazz™: blue vellum (*Pastel Vellum Papers*)
- solid Paper Pizazz™: red, blue (*Plain Brights*); yellow, brown, green (*Solid Muted Colors*); ivory (*Plain Pastels*); black (*Solid Jewel Tones*)
- yellow decorating chalk: Craf-T Products
- black pen: Zig® Millennium

left fingers

42

Boy Eating Cereal

- patterned Paper Pizazz™: spaghetti*, cereal (*Yummy Papers*); yellow gingham, blue dots (*Bright Tints*); lace (*Textured Papers*); purple stripes, green/purple diamonds (*Mixing Soft Patterns*)
- specialty Paper Pizazz™: silver* (by the sheet); sky blue vellum (*Pastel Vellum Papers*)
- solid Paper Pizazz™: ivory (*Plain Pastels*); black (*Solid Jewel Tones*)
- peach, pink, orange-red decorating chalks: Craf-T Products
- white pen: Pentel Milky Gel Roller
- black, red pens: Zig® Writer

left hand

left hand fingers

right hand fingers

left sleeve

inside back of bowl

rim of bowl

bowl front

placemat stripes

cereal (*Paper Pizazz™ Yummy Papers*); aqua (*Paper Pizazz™ 12"x12" Solid Pastel Papers*); red, blue, yellow (*Paper Pizazz™ Plain Brights*)

*This paper is also available by the sheet.

43

Bug Sitting on Flower

- patterned Paper Pizazz™: dark pink dots, purple gingham, yellow diamonds, green grid, green gingham (*Bright Tints*)
- solid Paper Pizazz™: purple, light orange (*Plain Brights*); white (*Plain Pastels*); black (*Solid Jewel Tones*)
- red, purple decorating chalks: Craf-T Products
- white pen: Pentel Milky Gel Roller
- black, red pens: Zig® Millennium

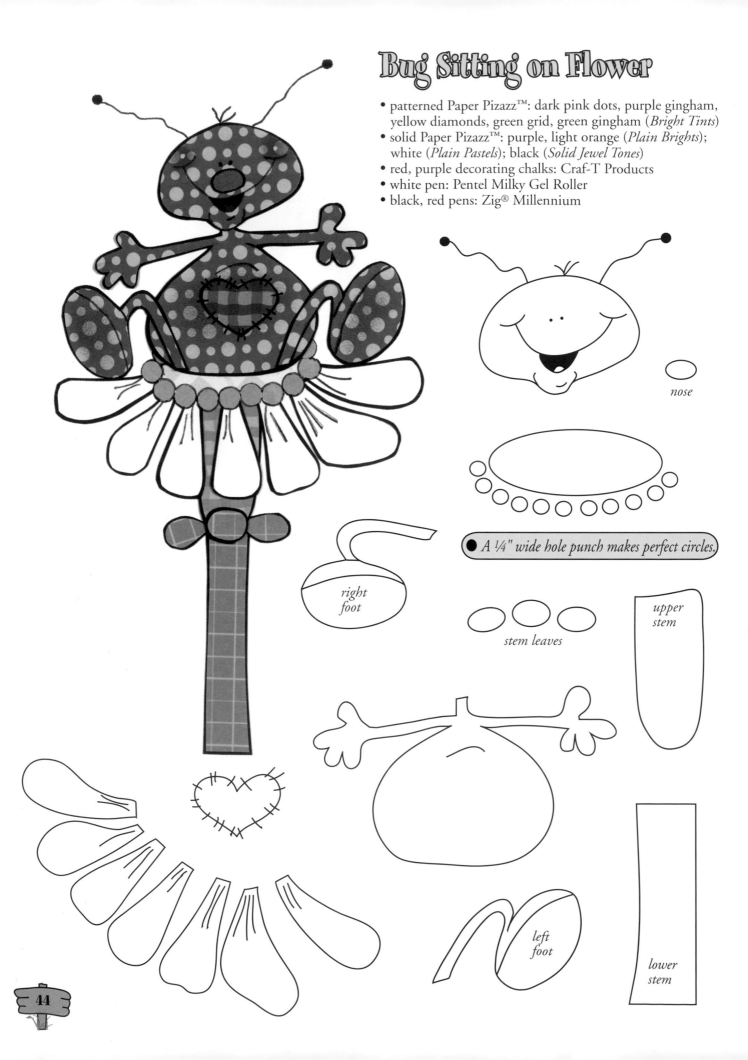

nose

● A ¼" wide hole punch makes perfect circles.

right foot

stem leaves

upper stem

left foot

lower stem

44

Bug Smiling

- patterned Paper Pizazz™: light green with dots* (*Light Great Backgrounds*)
- specialty Paper Pizazz™: pink vellum with dots (*Soft Patterns in Vellum*)
- solid Paper Pizazz™: light pink (*Plain Pastels*); black (*Solid Jewel Tones*)
- pink decorating chalk: Craf-T Products
- white pen: Pentel Milky Gel Roller
- black, red pens: Zig® Millennium

right hand

left hand

❣ *Use this colorful bug to adorn baby's first smile photos.*

left foot

left wing

OUR LiTTLE
CUTiE at
9 MONTHS OLD
JUNE 2001

right foot

right wing

pink/yellow plaid* (*Paper Pizazz™ Pastel Plaids*); yellow dots (*Paper Pizazz™ Soft Tints*); blue, yellow, white (*Paper Pizazz™ Plain Pastels*)

*This paper is also available by the sheet.

Bug Snorkeling

- patterned Paper Pizazz™: colorful stripes* (*Bright Great Backgrounds*); purple sponged* (*Pretty Papers*)
- specialty Paper Pizazz™: green vellum, purple vellum (*Pastel Vellum Papers*)
- solid Paper Pizazz™: green, red, yellow, blue (*Plain Brights*); black (*Solid Jewel Tones*)
- white pen: Pentel Milky Gel Roller
- black pen: Zig® Millennium

nose

vellum mask piece

right hand

left hand

right leg

left leg

pail stripe

shovel handle

● *A ¼" wide hole punch makes perfect circles.*

Bug with Crayon

- patterned Paper Pizazz™: yellow/lavender/green plaid* (*Pastel Plaids*); denim* (*Country*)
- solid Paper Pizazz™: lavender (*Solid Muted Colors*); light green, white (*Plain Pastels*); black (*Solid Jewel Tones*)
- black pen: Zig® Millennium

fingers

*This paper is also available by the sheet.

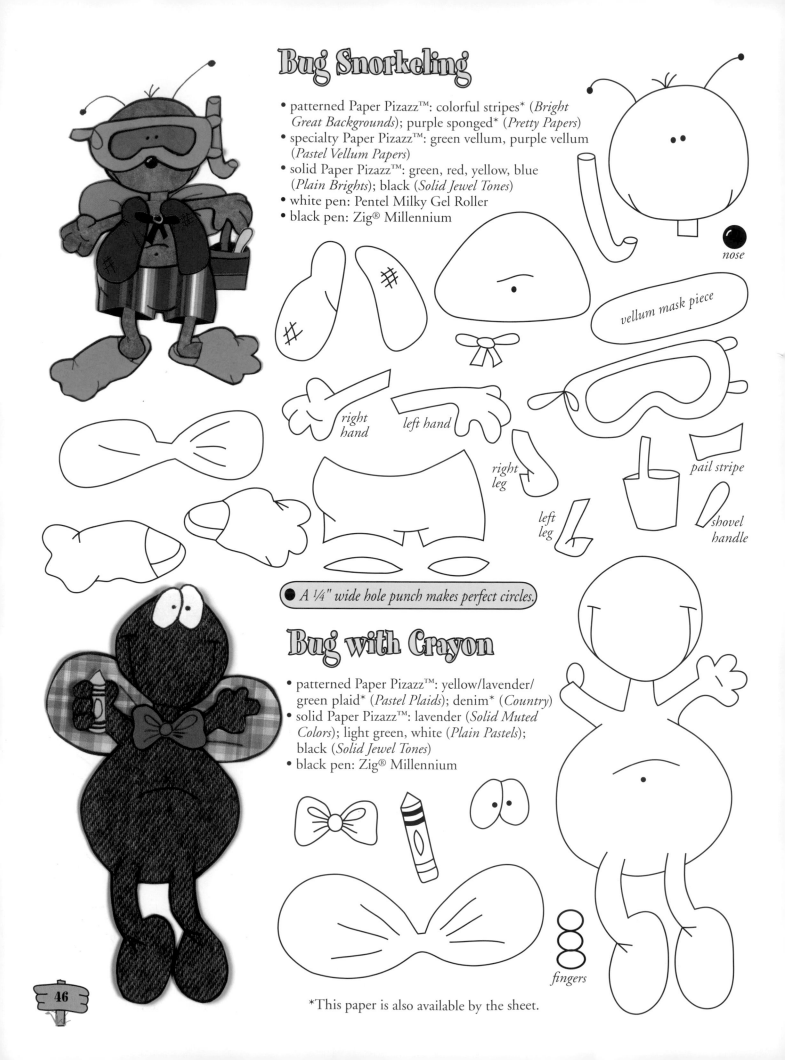

Bug with Glasses

- patterned Paper Pizazz™: green swirl* (*Pretty Papers*); forest green suede* (*Making Heritage Scrapbook Pages*)
- specialty Paper Pizazz™: green vellum, blue vellum (*Pastel Vellum Papers*)
- solid Paper Pizazz™: black (*Solid Jewel Tones*)
- dark pink decorating chalk: Craf-T Products
- black, red pens: Zig® Millennium

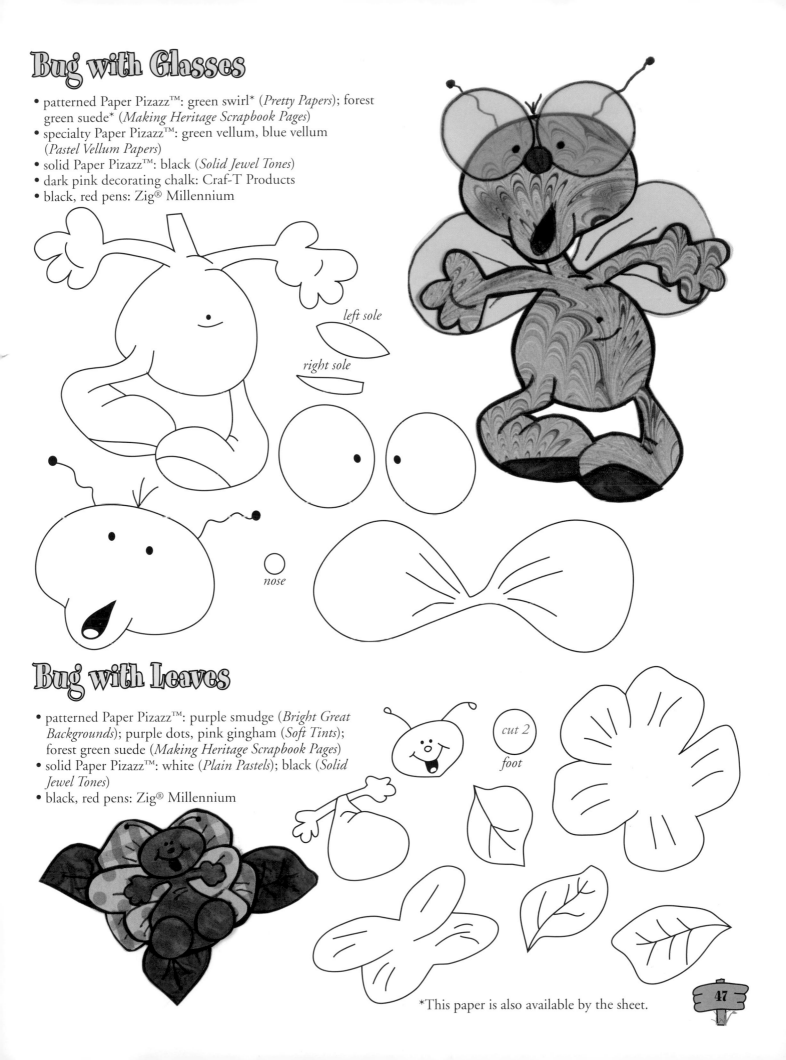

left sole

right sole

nose

Bug with Leaves

- patterned Paper Pizazz™: purple smudge (*Bright Great Backgrounds*); purple dots, pink gingham (*Soft Tints*); forest green suede (*Making Heritage Scrapbook Pages*)
- solid Paper Pizazz™: white (*Plain Pastels*); black (*Solid Jewel Tones*)
- black, red pens: Zig® Millennium

cut 2

foot

*This paper is also available by the sheet.

47

Bug with Paintbrush

right arm

left arm

hand cut 2

brush tip

right wing

left wing

- patterned Paper Pizazz™: lavender dots (*Soft Tints*); barnwood* (*Country*)
- specialty Paper Pizazz™: pink vellum (*Pastel Vellum Papers*)
- solid Paper Pizazz™: yellow, gray (*Solid Muted Colors*); black (*Solid Jewel Tones*)
- white pen: Pentel Milky Gel Roller
- black, red pens: Zig® Millennium

Bug with Paintbucket

- patterned Paper Pizazz™: green swirls, lavender dots (*Soft Tints*)
- specialty Paper Pizazz™: green vellum (*Pastel Vellum Papers*)
- solid Paper Pizazz™: yellow, gray (*Solid Muted Colors*); black (*Solid Jewel Tones*)
- pink decorating chalk: Craf-T Products
- black pen: Zig® Millennium

right wing

left wing

brush tip

brush

right hand fingers

*This paper is also available by the sheet.

Bunny

- patterned Paper Pizazz™: pink, peach smudge (*Light Great Backgrounds*); pink gingham (*Soft Tints*)
- solid Paper Pizazz™: black (*Solid Jewel Tones*)
- pink decorating chalk: Craf-T Products
- white pen: Pentel Milky Gel Roller
- black pen: Zig® Millennium

right paw

left paw

● *nose*

inner ears

❣ *Dark decorating chalk provides depth while light colors highlight special areas. Use pink to brighten the cheeks and blue for the water spout.*

Bunny in Watering Can

- patterned Paper Pizazz™: blue moiré, green swirl*, peach/pink brushstrokes (*Light Great Backgrounds*); lace netting (by the sheet)
- solid Paper Pizazz™: white (*Plain Pastels*); black (*Solid Jewel Tones*)
- blue, pink decorating chalks: Craf-T Products
- black pen: Sakura Gelly Roll

inner ears

cut 2

foot

*This paper is also available by the sheet.

Bunny with Carrot

- patterned Paper Pizazz™: peach flowers, green with white dot, blue plaid (*Mixing Soft Patterned Papers*); white moiré (by the sheet)
- solid Paper Pizazz™: pink, white (*Plain Pastels*); black (*Solid Jewel Tones*)
- pink decorating chalk: Craf-T Products
- white pen: Pentel Milky Gel Roller
- black pen: Sakura Gelly Roll

right foot

left foot

right paw

left paw

Bunny with Heart Lollipop

- patterned Paper Pizazz™: brown velvet (*"Velvet" Backgrounds*); dark pink with dots, dark pink swirls (*Bright Tints*)
- solid Paper Pizazz™: dark pink (*Plain Pastels*); tan (*Solid Muted Colors*); black (*Solid Jewel Tones*)
- pink decorating chalk: Craf-T Products
- white pen: Pentel Milky Gel Roller
- black pen: Zig® Writer

or use a 1" wide heart punch

nose

tail

50

*This paper is also available by the sheet.

Bunny with Vest

nose

tail

inner ears

right paw

left paw

- patterned Paper Pizazz™: green/yellow/pink plaid* (*Pastel Plaids*); green swirls (*Soft Tints*); tri-dots on light pink* (*Light Great Backgrounds*)
- solid Paper Pizazz™: yellow, dark pink (*Plain Pastels*); black (*Solid Jewel Tones*)
- pink decorating chalk: Craf-T Products
- white pen: Pentel Milky Gel Roller
- black pen: Zig® Writer

Butterflies with Pencil

- patterned Paper Pizazz™: yellow check (*Bright Tints*); lavender dots, peach tri-dots*, green dots (*Dots, Checks, Plaids & Stripes*)
- solid Paper Pizazz™: lavender, yellow, light green (*Plain Pastels*); black, gray (*Solid Jewel Tones*)
- pink decorating chalk: Craf-T Products
- white pen: Pentel Milky Gel Roller
- black, red pens: Zig® Writer

back butterfly pieces

front butterfly pieces

hands

*This paper is also available by the sheet.

Butterfly

- patterned Paper Pizazz™: purple/pink swirl, purple/black swirl, purple swirl* (*Bright Great Backgrounds*)
- solid Paper Pizazz™: black (*Solid Jewel Tones*)
- black pen: Zig® Writer

ivy (*Paper Pizazz™ 12x12 by the sheet*); vellum swirls* (*Paper Pizazz™ Vellum Papers*); medium blue, lavender (*Paper Pizazz™ 12x12 Solid Pastel Papers*)

Butterfly on Paintbrush

- patterned Paper Pizazz™: barnwood* (*Country*); purple sponged* (*Pretty Papers*)
- specialty Paper Pizazz™: striped blue vellum (*Soft Patterns in Vellum*)
- solid Paper Pizazz™: lavender (*Plain Pastels*); black, gray (*Solid Jewel Tones*)
- pink decorating chalk: Craf-T Products
- white pen: Pentel Milky Gel Roller
- black, red pens: Zig® Writer

lower
cut 2

upper
cut 2

inner wings

This paper is also available by the sheet.

Butterfly with Banner

- patterned Paper Pizazz™: Best Bud's Companion–purple (*A Girl's Scrapbook*); crushed teal, multi-colored with black (*Bright Great Backgrounds*)
- solid Paper Pizazz™: black (*Solid Jewel Tones*)
- pink pen: Pentel Milky Gel Roller
- black pen: Zig® Writer

cut 2

outer lower wing

inner upper wing

cut 2

outer upper wing

cut 2

inner lower wing

fingers

right inner banner

right end of banner

left inner banner

left end of banner

Spring Brings Smiles

Butterfly Side View

- patterned Paper Pizazz™: purple chevrons, blue with purple tri-dot, pink swirls (*Soft Tints*)
- solid Paper Pizazz™: black (*Solid Jewel Tones*)
- white pen: Pentel Milky Gel Roller
- black pen: Zig® Writer

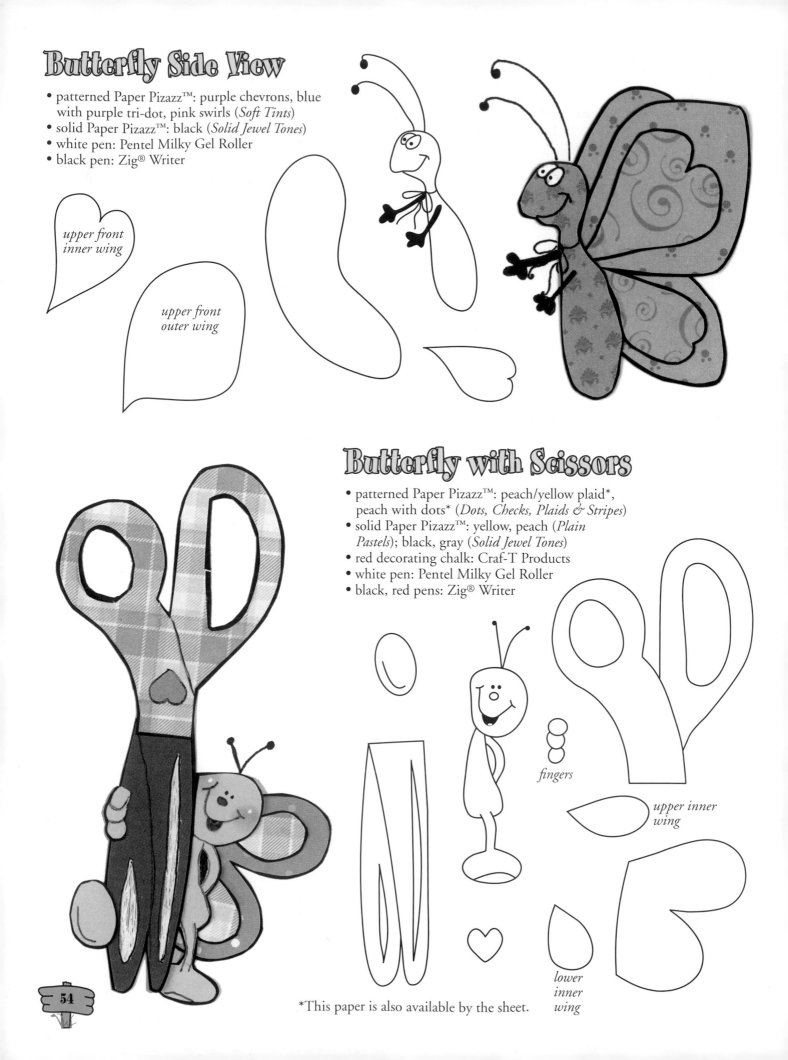

upper front inner wing

upper front outer wing

Butterfly with Scissors

- patterned Paper Pizazz™: peach/yellow plaid*, peach with dots* (*Dots, Checks, Plaids & Stripes*)
- solid Paper Pizazz™: yellow, peach (*Plain Pastels*); black, gray (*Solid Jewel Tones*)
- red decorating chalk: Craf-T Products
- white pen: Pentel Milky Gel Roller
- black, red pens: Zig® Writer

fingers

upper inner wing

lower inner wing

*This paper is also available by the sheet.

Butterfly with "Smile" Bag

- patterned Paper Pizazz™: multicolored green/blue/gold, blue brushed, purple brushed (*Bright Great Backgrounds*)
- solid Paper Pizazz™: goldenrod, green (*Plain Brights*); white (*Plain Pastels*); black (*Solid Jewel Tones*)
- white, yellow-orange decorating chalks: Craf-T Products
- blue pen: Sakura Gelly Roll
- black pen: Zig® Writer

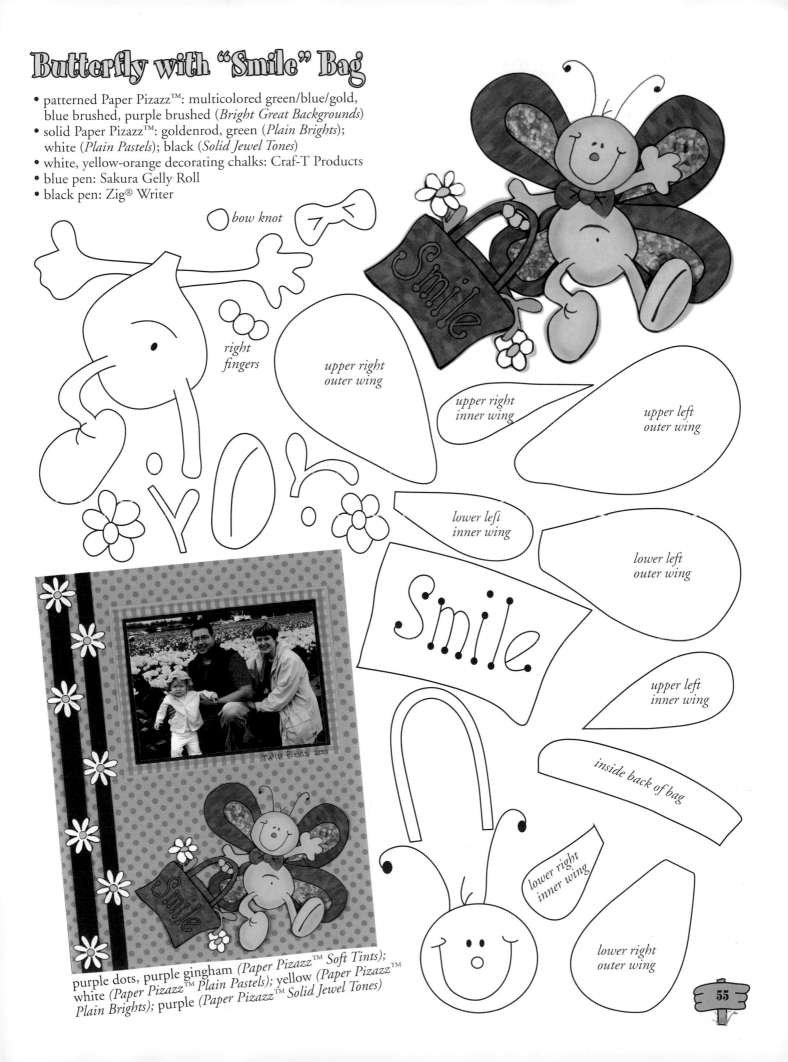

bow knot

right fingers

upper right outer wing

upper right inner wing

upper left outer wing

lower left inner wing

lower left outer wing

Smile

upper left inner wing

inside back of bag

lower right inner wing

lower right outer wing

Tulip fields 2001

purple dots, purple gingham (*Paper Pizazz™ Soft Tints*); white (*Paper Pizazz™ Plain Pastels*); yellow (*Paper Pizazz™ Plain Brights*); purple (*Paper Pizazz™ Solid Jewel Tones*)

Candy Train

- patterned Paper Pizazz™: gum drops, graham crackers, jelly beans, chocolate, peppermints, popcorn, gum drops (*Yummy Papers*); white dots on green, red & green stripe* (*Red & Green Coordinating Colors*™); white dot on red*, red & white stripes* (*Ho, Ho, Ho!!!*)
- solid Paper Pizazz™: red, green, yellow (*Plain Brights*); white (*Plain Pastels*); black (*Solid Jewel Tones*)
- brown decorating chalk: Craf-T Products
- black, red pens: Zig® Millennium

caboose

caboose top

caboose

caboose top

caboose

Jelly Beans

wheel link

cut 3

cut 3

♣ *Use a very simple background paper behind the train so each detail will shine through.*

wheel | *cut 7 from gum drops*

cut 10 green, 2 red

cut 3 | jelly beans | *cut 3*

train links

cut 2

white dot on red*, white dots on green, red & green dots*, Christmas candy* (*Paper Pizazz*™ *Christmas Time*); white (*Paper Pizazz*™ *12"x12" Plain Pastels*); black (*Paper Pizazz*™ *12"x12" Black & White Coordinating Colors*™)

*This paper is also available by the sheet.

Chocolate

chocolate pieces

booth top

engine wheel
cut 2 from
peppermints

cut 5 from
gum drops

cut 7 green,
4 red

wheel links

train link

conductor's booth

engine border

engine

Sugartown
EXPRESS

popcorn kernels

cut 2

cut 2

gum drops

engine
nose

engine nose

marshmallow pieces

cut 2

The "choo" was created by an alphabet template
(*Fat Caps*, Francis Meyer®); black pen (*Marvy®
Uchida Glitter Gel Excel*).

Candy Corns

- patterned Paper Pizazz™: candy corn* (*Holidays & Seasons*)
- solid Paper Pizazz™: yellow, red (*Plain Brights*); white (*Plain Pastels*); black (*Solid Jewel Tones*)
- white pen: Pentel Milky Gel Roller
- black, red pens: Zig® Millennium

cut 3

cut 3

cut 3

nose
cut 3

cut 6

Canning Jars

- patterned Paper Pizazz™: green/black plaid, blue/black plaid, green/yellow plaid (*Jewel Plaids*)
- solid Paper Pizazz™: red, yellow (*Plain Brights*); white (*Plain Pastels*); blue, black (*Solid Jewel Tones*)
- white, black decorating chalks: Craf-T Products
- black pen: Sakura Gelly Roll

*This paper is also available by the sheet.

Cat with Book

- patterned Paper Pizazz™: burgundy with wheat, tan diamonds (*Mixing Jewel Patterned Papers*); rosebuds, blue plaid (*Mixing Soft Patterned Papers*)
- solid Paper Pizazz™: light yellow, ivory (*Plain Pastels*); black, brown (*Solid Jewel Tones*)
- blue decorating chalk: Craf-T Products
- yellow pen: Zig® Writer
- white pen: Pentel Milky Gel Roller
- black pen: Sakura Gelly Roll

A GOOD BOOK

A GOOD BOOK

❣ *Make your page even more special by writing your child's favorite book title on the front of the book piece.*

Cat with Bow

- patterned Paper Pizazz™: cookies (by the sheet); green checks* (*Hunter Green Coordinating Colors*™)
- solid Paper Pizazz™: ivory (*Plain Pastels*); black (*Solid Jewel Tones*)
- pink, brown decorating chalks: Craf-T Products
- white pen: Pentel Milky Gel Roller
- black pen: Sakura Gelly Roll

Cat with Fluffy Chest

- patterned Paper Pizazz™: potato chips (*Yummy Papers*); animal crackers* (*Child's Play*); girl power companion* (*A Girl's Scrapbook*)
- solid Paper Pizazz™: black (*Solid Jewel Tones*)
- pink decorating chalk: Craf-T Products
- white pen: Pentel Milky Gel Roller
- black pen: Sakura Gelly Roll

*This paper is also available by the sheet.

Cat with Jack-o-Lantern

- patterned Paper Pizazz™: black swirl (*Bright Great Backgrounds*); black/orange gingham (by the sheet)
- solid Paper Pizazz™: bright green, yellow, blue (*Plain Brights*); black, hunter green (*Solid Jewel Tones*)
- orange, blue, purple, lime green decorating chalks: Craf-T Products
- white, yellow pens: Pentel Milky Gel Roller
- red pen: Marvy® Uchida Gel Sparkles
- black pen: Sakura Gelly Roll

nose

Cat with Kitten

- patterned Paper Pizazz™: brown & gold swirl*, red moiré* (*Black & White Photos*); handmade tan, handmade blue, handmade brown (*"Handmade" Papers*)
- solid Paper Pizazz™: ivory (*Plain Pastels*); black (*Solid Jewel Tones*)
- white pen: Pentel Milky Gel Roller
- black pen: Sakura Gelly Roll

kitten stripes

*This paper is also available by the sheet.

61

Cat with Vest

- patterned Paper Pizazz™: brown velvet ("*Velvet*" *Backgrounds*); blue & yellow plaid, yellow with lavender dots (by the sheet)
- solid Paper Pizazz™: ivory (*Plain Pastels*); black (*Solid Jewel Tones*)
- brown, pink decorating chalks: Craf-T Products
- white pen: Pentel Milky Gel Roller
- black pen: Sakura Gelly Roll

left vest

right vest

Chick Painting Eggs

- patterned Paper Pizazz™: yellow roses* (*Romantic Papers*); cork board* (*School Days*); barnwood* (*Country*); yellow squiggle lines, pink flowers, green chevrons, purple gingham, green swirls, blue dots (*Soft Tints*)
- solid Paper Pizazz™: black, gray (*Solid Jewel Tones*)
- black pen: Zig® Writer

left fingers

left foot

right foot

right fingers

beak

← *cut*

brush tip

right back fingers

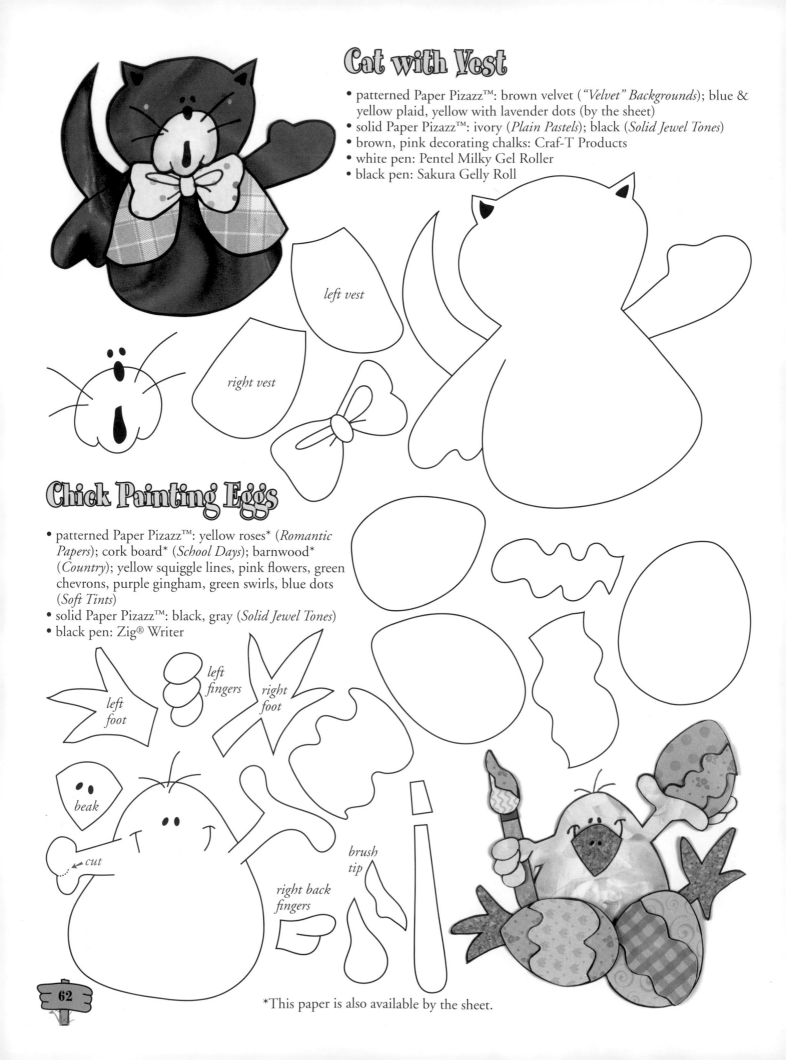

*This paper is also available by the sheet.

Child Giving Self Haircut

- patterned Paper Pizazz™: blue with yellow swirls, green/blue draped fabric, tan with black chevrons, black/tan tiles (*Mixing Jewel Patterned Papers*); yellow swirls (*Bright Tints*)
- specialty Paper Pizazz™: blue vellum (*Pastel Vellum Papers*); silver* (by the sheet)
- solid Paper Pizazz™: goldenrod (*Plain Brights*); ivory (*Plain Pastels*); black (*Solid Jewel Tones*)
- peach, pink, white, orange-red decorating chalks: Craf-T Products
- white pen: Pentel Milky Gel Roller
- black, orange pens: Zig® Writer

left hand

right hand

shirt

sleeves

right back apron

left back apron

right foot

left foot

*This paper is also available by the sheet.

Child in Bat Costume

- patterned Paper Pizazz™: purple scales (*Mixing Jewel Patterned Papers*); burgundy calla lilies (*Collage Papers*); handmade black (*"Handmade" Papers*)
- solid Paper Pizazz™: pale yellow (*Plain Pastels*); black (*Solid Jewel Tones*)
- peach, pink, white, orange-red decorating chalks: Craf-T Products
- white pen: Pentel Milky Gel Roller
- black, red pens: Zig® Writer

bow knot

cut 2

right wing

right hand

left wing

right sole

left hand

left sole

purple sponged* (*Paper Pizazz™ Pretty Papers*); black, purple (*Paper Pizazz™ Solid Jewel Tones*); trick or treat (*Paper Pizazz™ Title Punch-Outs™*)

Child in Bathrobe with Puppy

- patterned Paper Pizazz™: blue plaid, green with white dots (*Mixing Soft Patterned Papers*); brown/tan diamonds (*Mixing Jewel Patterned Papers*); white lace (*Textured Papers*)
- solid Paper Pizazz™: ivory (*Plain Pastels*); black (*Solid Jewel Tones*)
- pink, peach, orange-red decorating chalks: Craf-T Products
- white pen: Pentel Milky Gel Roller
- black, red pens: Zig® Writer

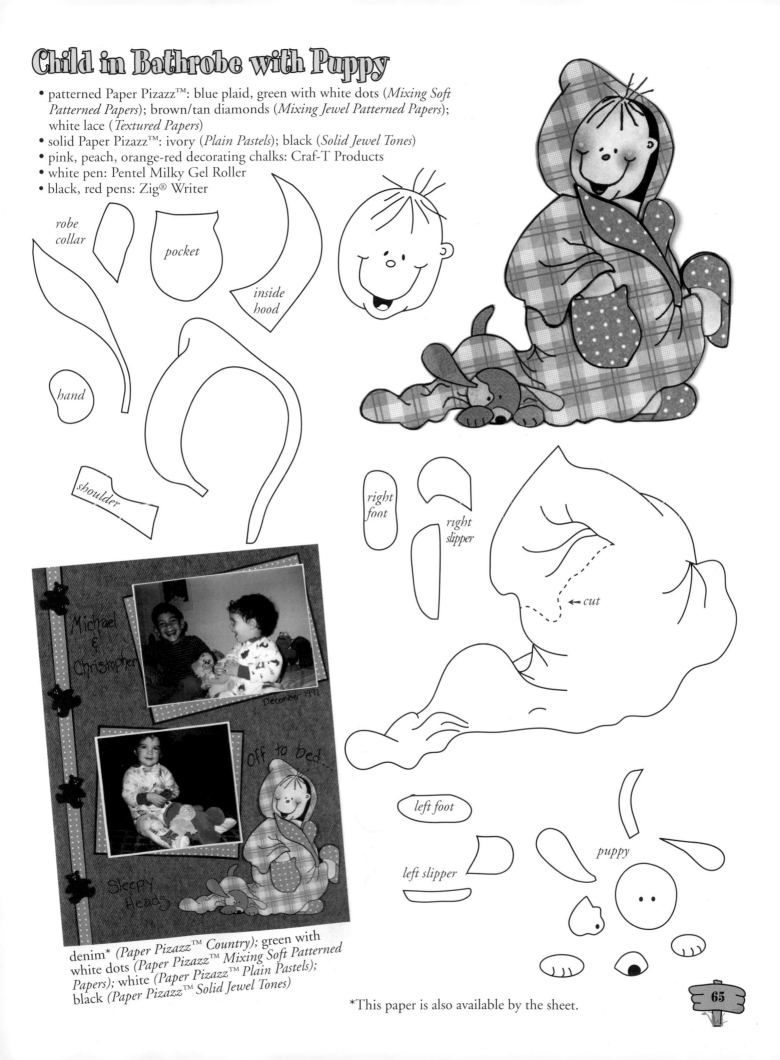

robe collar

pocket

inside hood

hand

shoulder

right foot

right slipper

← cut

Michael & Christopher

December 1991

Off to bed...

Sleepy Heads

left foot

left slipper

puppy

denim* (*Paper Pizazz™ Country*); green with white dots (*Paper Pizazz™ Mixing Soft Patterned Papers*); white (*Paper Pizazz™ Plain Pastels*); black (*Paper Pizazz™ Solid Jewel Tones*)

*This paper is also available by the sheet.

65

Child in Bunny Suit

- patterned Paper Pizazz™: blue checks & swirls, girl power* (*A Girl's Scrapbook*); burlap* (*Country*); white lace (*Textured Papers*)
- solid Paper Pizazz™: ivory (*Plain Pastels*); black (*Solid Jewel Tones*)
- pink, peach, white, orange-red, blue-purple, black decorating chalks: Craf-T Products
- white pen: Pentel Milky Gel Roller
- black, red pens: Zig® Writer

right arm

bow knot

tail

cut 3

basket center

left arm

inner ears

left sole

right sole

yellow stars, blue check (*Paper Pizazz™ Lisa Williams Blue, Yellow & Green*); white, dark pink, yellow, blue (*Paper Pizazz™ Plain Pastels*)

*This paper is also available by the sheet.

Child in Butterfly Suit

- patterned Paper Pizazz™: blue dots, blue flowers, green with yellow tri-dots, yellow with green tri-dots, yellow squiggle lines (*Soft Tints*)
- solid Paper Pizazz™: ivory (*Plain Pastels*); black (*Solid Jewel Tones*)
- peach, pink, white, orange-red decorating chalks: Craf-T Products
- white pen: Pentel Milky Gel Roller
- black, red: Zig® Writer

left hand

right hand

right leg

left leg

upper wing

cut 2

ankle ruffles

left sleeve

lower wing

cut 2

right sleeve

lower inner wing

cut 2

upper inner wing

cut 2

Child in Fall Costume

- patterned Paper Pizazz™: botanical collage with border, green botonical collage with border (*Collage Papers*); barnwood*, burlap* (*Country*); gold sponged stars* (*A Woman's Scrapbook*)
- solid Paper Pizazz™: red (*Plain Brights*); ivory (*Plain Pastels*); black (*Solid Jewel Tones*)
- peach, pink, white, orange-red decorating chalks: Craf-T Products
- white pen: Pentel Milky Gel Roller
- black, red pens: Zig® Writer

twig leaves

right hand

left hand

apples

inner basket back

arm

cut 2

*This paper is also available by the sheet.

67

Child in Snowsuit with Broom

- patterned Paper Pizazz™: clouds* (*Vacation*); snowflakes (by the sheet); barnwood* (*Country*)
- solid Paper Pizazz™: ivory (*Plain Pastels*); brown (*Solid Muted Colors*); black (*Solid Jewel Tones*)
- peach, pink, white decorating chalks: Craf-T Products
- white pen: Pentel Milky Gel Roller
- black, red: Zig® Writer

left fingers

left hand

bow knot

broom band

right arm

left arm

right hand

soles

*This paper is also available by the sheet.

Christmas Tree

- patterned Paper Pizazz™: yellow swirls (*Bright Tints*)
- solid Paper Pizazz™: green, brown (*Solid Muted Colors*); black (*Solid Jewel Tones*)
- dark green, light green, light brown, white decorating chalks: Craf-T Products
- white, pink pens: Pentel Milky Gel Roller
- black pen: Zig® Writer

Cloud Pull Toy

- patterned Paper Pizazz™: clouds* (*Vacation*)
- solid Paper Pizazz™: yellow (*Solid Muted Colors*); blue (*Plain Pastels*); black (*Solid Jewel Tones*)
- red decorating chalk: Craf-T Products
- black, red pens: Zig® Millennium

cut 2

*This paper is also available by the sheet.

Clown

- patterned Paper Pizazz™: black with blue dots, black with pink/blue stripes, pink with black tri-dots, purple with black dots (*Bold & Bright*)
- solid Paper Pizazz™: white (*Plain Pastels*); black (*Solid Jewel Tones*)
- orange-red decorating chalk: Craf-T Products
- white pen: Pentel Milky Gel Roller
- black, red pens: Zig® Writer

right hair

right sleeve

left hair

right hand

left hand

Clown Juggling

- patterned Paper Pizazz™: black with dots*, red with dots* (*Bright Great Backgrounds*); red & white stripes (*Red & White Coordinating Colors*™)
- solid Paper Pizazz™: red, orange, yellow, green (*Plain Brights*); white (*Plain Pastels*); black (*Solid Jewel Tones*)
- black decorating chalk: Craf-T Products
- white pen: Pentel Milky Gel Roller
- black pen: Zig® Millennium

ribbon folds

cut 3

hair

nose

legs

hands

right pocket

left pocket

70

*This paper is also available by the sheet.

Clown Jack-in-the-Box

- patterned Paper Pizazz™: school tartan* (*School Days*); green stripes, yellow diamonds (*Bright Tints*)
- solid Paper Pizazz™: red, orange, yellow, green (*Plain Brights*); white (*Plain Pastels*); black (*Solid Jewel Tones*)
- black decorating chalk: Craf-T Products
- black, red pens: Zig® Millennium

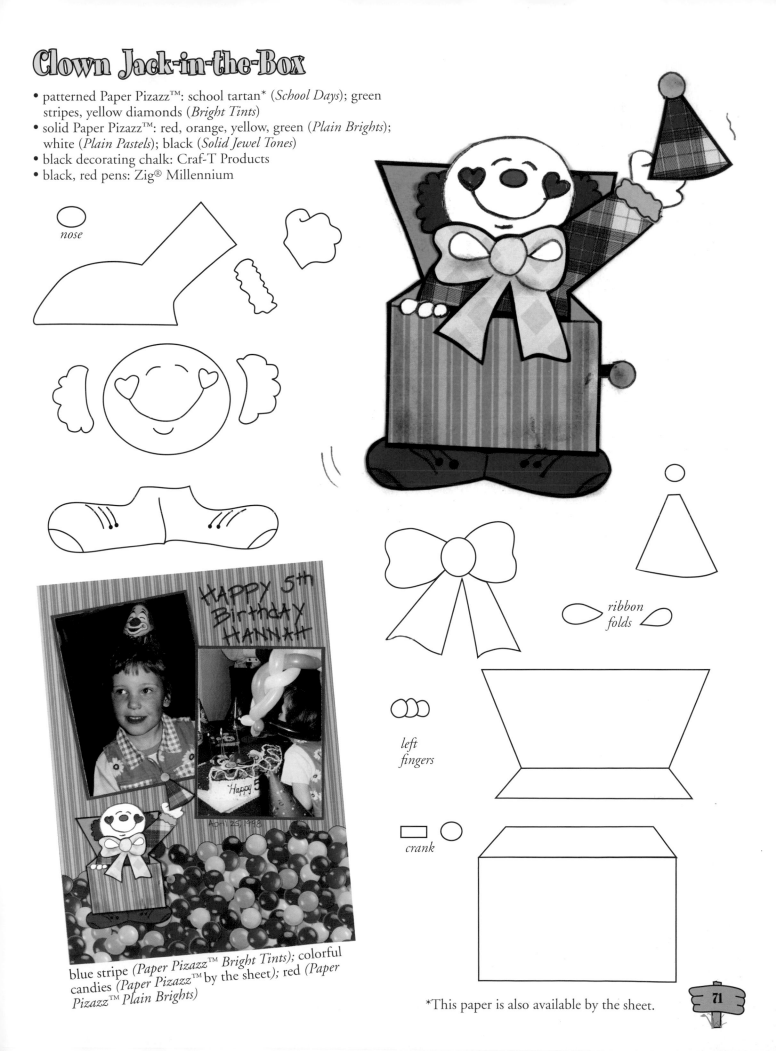

nose

ribbon folds

left fingers

crank

blue stripe (*Paper Pizazz™ Bright Tints*); colorful candies (*Paper Pizazz™ by the sheet*); red (*Paper Pizazz™ Plain Brights*)

*This paper is also available by the sheet.

Clown with Ball

- patterned Paper Pizazz™: yellow diamonds (*Bright Tints*); colorful stripes* (*Birthday*)
- solid Paper Pizazz™: red, orange, yellow, green, aqua (*Plain Brights*); white, dark pink (*Plain Pastels*); black (*Solid Jewel Tones*)
- black, red, purple decorating chalks: Craf-T Products
- black pen: Zig® Millennium

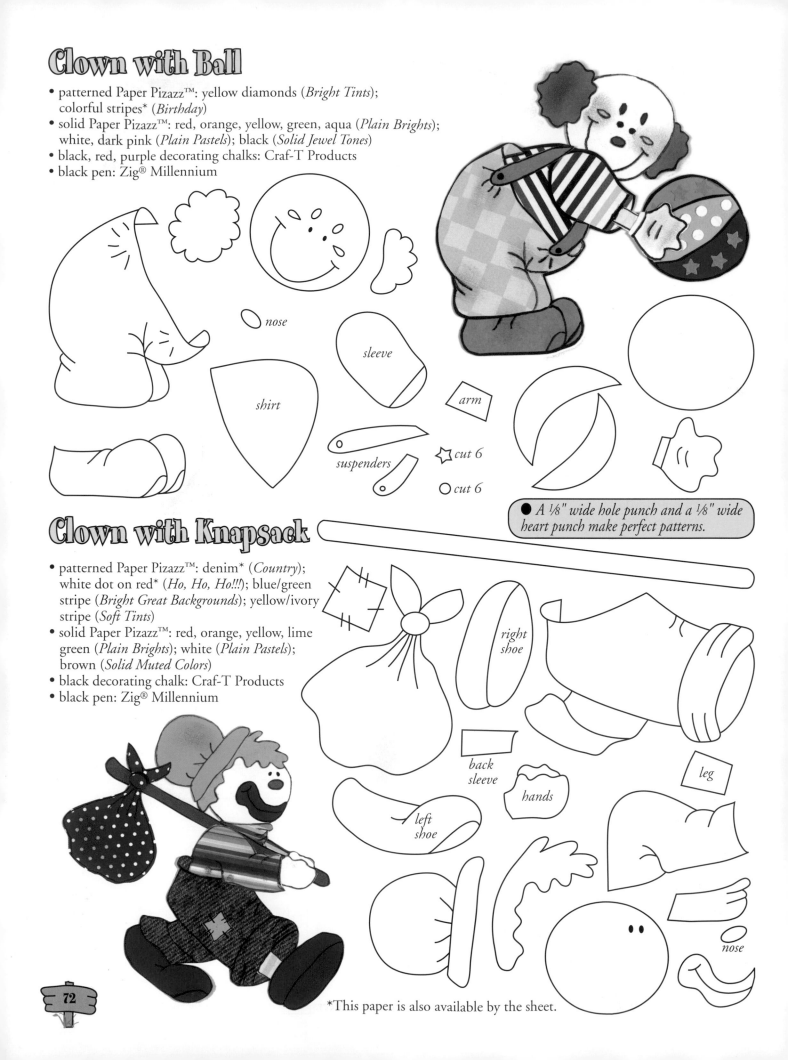

nose

sleeve

shirt

arm

suspenders

☆ *cut 6*

○ *cut 6*

● *A ⅛" wide hole punch and a ⅛" wide heart punch make perfect patterns.*

Clown with Knapsack

- patterned Paper Pizazz™: denim* (*Country*); white dot on red* (*Ho, Ho, Ho!!!*); blue/green stripe (*Bright Great Backgrounds*); yellow/ivory stripe (*Soft Tints*)
- solid Paper Pizazz™: red, orange, yellow, lime green (*Plain Brights*); white (*Plain Pastels*); brown (*Solid Muted Colors*)
- black decorating chalk: Craf-T Products
- black pen: Zig® Millennium

right shoe

back sleeve

leg

hands

left shoe

nose

*This paper is also available by the sheet.

Computer

- patterned Paper Pizazz™: blue smudge (*Bright Great Backgrounds*)
- solid Paper Pizazz™: white (*Plain Pastels*); black (*Solid Jewel Tones*)
- red decorating chalk: Craf-T Products
- black, red pens: Zig® Millennium

Cow Jumping Over Moon

- patterned Paper Pizazz™: black with white dots* (*Black & White Coordinating Colors*™)
- solid Paper Pizazz™: peach, yellow (*Solid Muted Colors*); red (*Plain Brights*); white (*Plain Pastels*)
- red decorating chalk: Craf-T Products
- white pen: Pentel Milky Gel Roller
- black, red pens: Zig® Millennium

head spots

spots

ears

horns

collar

cut 3 →

front hooves

back hooves

tail

*This paper is also available by the sheet.

Daisies

- patterned Paper Pizazz™: yellow dot, green gingham (*Bright Tints*)
- specialty Paper Pizazz™: lavender vellum (*Pastel Vellum Papers*)
- solid Paper Pizazz™: white (*Plain Pastels*); black (*Solid Jewel Tones*)
- red decorating chalk: Craf-T Products
- white pen: Pentel Milky Gel Roller
- black pen: Sakura Gelly Roll

Dinosaur

- patterned Paper Pizazz™: rhinosaurus skin, palm leaves (*Wild Things*); white lace (*Textured Papers*)
- solid Paper Pizazz™: black (*Solid Jewel Tones*)
- white, black, orange-red decorating chalks: Craf-T Products
- white pen: Pentel Milky Gel Roller
- black pen: Zig® Writer

right leaf

front horn

left leaf

center leaf

left horn

right horn

Dinosaur in Cave

- patterned Paper Pizazz™: black swirls, blue mix, blue/gold/green speckled (*Bright Great Backgrounds*); grass (by the sheet)
- solid Paper Pizazz™: black (*Solid Jewel Tones*)
- black pen: Zig® Writer

tummy

tummy

Dinosaur Running

- patterned Paper Pizazz™: green swirls (*Mixing Soft Patterned Papers*); purple scales (*Mixed Jewel Patterned Papers*)
- solid Paper Pizazz™: black (*Solid Jewel Tones*)
- green decorating chalk: Craf-T Products
- black pen: Zig® Writer

cut

← *cut*

cut →

Dinosaur Standing on Back Legs

- patterned Paper Pizazz™: blue textured, purple swirls (*Bright Great Backgrounds*)
- solid Paper Pizazz™: black (*Solid Jewel Tones*)
- black pen: Zig® Writer

back foot

tummy

front foot

cut

cut

CHRISTOPHER AT THE PREHISTORIC GARDENS

ferns* *(Paper Pizazz™ Great Outdoors)*; brown, navy blue *(Paper Pizazz™ Solid Jewel Tones)*; white *(Paper Pizazz™ Plain Pastels)*

*This paper is also available by the sheet.

Dog, Cat, Mouse & Present

- patterned Paper Pizazz™: yellow squiggle lines (*Soft Tints*); handmade brown, handmade gray (*"Handmade" Papers*); cork board* (*School Days*); dots on red* (*Bright Great Backgrounds*); pink plaid* (*Pastel Plaids*)
- solid Paper Pizazz™: ivory, white, light blue (*Plain Pastels*); tan (*Solid Muted Colors*); black (*Solid Jewel Tones*)
- brown, pink decorating chalks: Craf-T Products
- white pen: Pentel Milky Gel Roller
- black, green pens: Sakura Gelly Roll

jaw & tummy

collar

left paw

back paw

gray spots

ribbon

face spots

arm

paw

tie

vest

NO PEEKING!

tail

spots

cat tummy

left sole

right sole

*This paper is also available by the sheet.

Dog with Patches

- patterned Paper Pizazz™: handmade cream ("*Handmade*" *Papers*); brown plaid* (*Great Outdoors*)
- solid Paper Pizazz™: black (*Solid Jewel Tones*)
- brown, pink decorating chalks: Craf-T Products
- white pen: Pentel Milky Gel Roller
- black pen: Sakura Gelly Roll

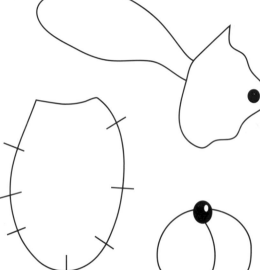

❣ *This little doggie would work perfectly with your pet photos or on a birthday party page.*

brown plaid* (*Paper Pizazz™ Great Outdoors*); barnwood* (*Paper Pizazz™ Country*); black, brown (*Paper Pizazz™ Solid Jewel Tones*)

*This paper is also available by the sheet.

Duck Pull Toy

- patterned Paper Pizazz™: yellow dots, blue gingham, pink gingham (*Soft Tints*); barnwood* (*Country*)
- solid Paper Pizazz™: peach, white (*Plain Pastels*); black (*Solid Jewel Tones*)
- pink decorating chalk: Craf-T Products
- black pen: Zig® Millennium

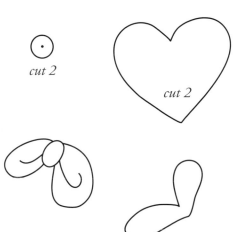

cut 2

cut 2

● *A ¼" wide hole punch makes perfect circles.*

Brynn Rose August 1, 1999

pink/yellow plaid (*Paper Pizazz™ by the sheet*); white, pink (*Paper Pizazz™ Plain Pastels*)

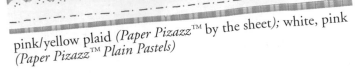

*This paper is also available by the sheet.

Elf with Tree Ornaments

- patterned Paper Pizazz™: green with stars* (*Dots, Checks, Plaids & Stripes*); red/yellow gingham, red with yellow dots (*Bright Tints*)
- solid Paper Pizazz™: peach, yellow (*Solid Muted Colors*); purple, red, blue, black (*Solid Jewel Tones*)
- red decorating chalk: Craf-T Products
- white pen: Pentel Milky Gel Roller
- black, red pens: Zig® Millennium

left arm

right arm

Fairy behind Pumpkins

- patterned Paper Pizazz™: orange dot (*Orange & Black Coordinating Colors*™)
- specialty Paper Pizazz™: blue vellum (*Pastel Vellum Papers*)
- solid Paper Pizazz™: ivory, yellow (*Plain Pastels*); green, black (*Solid Jewel Tones*)
- peach, pink decorating chalks: Craf-T Products
- white pen: Pentel Milky Gel Roller
- black pen: Sakura Gelly Roll

left wing

right wing

fingers

collar

80

*This paper is also available by the sheet.

Firecrackers & Stars

- patterned Paper Pizazz™: yellow swirls (*Bright Tints*); red pinstripe*, red with stars*, navy tri-dots (*Dots, Checks, Plaids & Stripes*); red moiré* (*Black & White Photos*)
- solid Paper Pizazz™: red, blue (*Plain Brights*); white (*Plain Pastels*); black (*Solid Jewel Tones*)
- red pen: Zig® Scroll & Brush
- black pen: Zig® Writer

upper pinstripe

stars stripe

white stripe

lower pinstripe

white stripe

navy tri-dot stripe

Yankee Doodle Dandy... Gary really got into the 4th of July spirit this year. We went to the parade and fireworks this year. '97

lower tri-dot stripe

lower white stripe

red tri-dots (*Paper Pizazz™ Stripes, Checks & Dots*); navy pinstripe* (*Paper Pizazz™ Dots, Checks, Plaids & Stripes*); white (*Paper Pizazz™ Plain Pastels*)

*This paper is also available by the sheet.

Fish & Coral

- patterned Paper Pizazz™: yellow diamonds, pink swirls (*Soft Tints*)
- solid Paper Pizazz™: peach, light blue, aqua green (*Solid Muted Colors*); white (*Plain Pastels*)
- pink decorating chalk: Craf-T Products
- black pen: Zig® Millennium

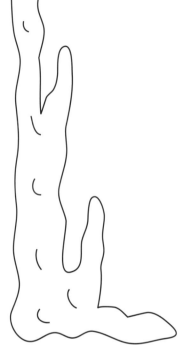

cut 7

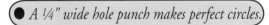

● *A ¼" wide hole punch makes perfect circles.*

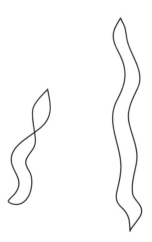

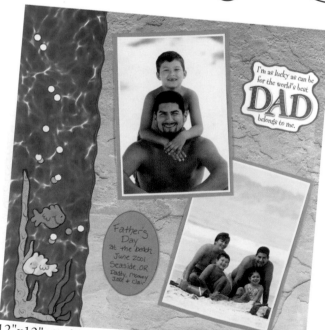

❣ *Wouldn't this adorable pattern be just the thing for your baby in the bath photos?*

12"x12" pool water, 12"x12" sandstone (*Paper Pizazz™ by the sheet*); brown (*Paper Pizazz™ 12"x12" Brown & White Coordinating Colors™*); blue (*Paper Pizazz™ Solid Muted Colors*); saying (*Paper Pizazz™ Punch-Outs™ Sayings #3*)

Fish in Bowl

- patterned Paper Pizazz™: peach tri-dots* (*Light Great Backgrounds*); yellow/ivory stripes, yellow gingham (*Soft Tints*); grass (by the sheet)
- specialty Paper Pizazz™: white vellum, blue vellum (*Pastel Vellum Papers*)
- solid Paper Pizazz™: white (*Plain Pastels*); black (*Solid Jewel Tones*)
- red decorating chalk: Craf-T Products
- black pen: Zig® Writer

● *¼" wide and ⅜" wide hole punches make perfect patterns.*

cut 2

large bubbles* (*Paper Pizazz™ Childhood*); bubbles* (*Paper Pizazz™ Baby*); blue vellem (*Paper Pizazz™ Pastel Vellum Papers*); navy blue (*Paper Pizazz™ Solid Jewel Tones*)

*This paper is also available by the sheet.

- patterned Paper Pizazz™: blue dots, yellow swirls, red with yellow swirls, red with yellow grid (*Bright Tints*)
- solid Paper Pizazz™: white (*Plain Pastels*); black (*Solid Jewel Tones*)
- white, gray decorating chalks: Craf-T Products
- orange pen: Zig® Scroll & Brush
- black pen: Zig® Writer

Frog with Daisy #1

- patterned Paper Pizazz™: fir trees (*Vacation*)
- solid Paper Pizazz™: yellow (*Vacation*); white (*Plain Pastels*); black (*Solid Jewel Tones*)
- black pen: Sakura Gelly Roll

right fingers

left fingers

Frog with Daisy #2

- patterned Paper Pizazz™: green with dots*, green checks* (*Hunter Green Coordinating Colors*™)
- solid Paper Pizazz™: white, light yellow (*Plain Pastels*); black, green (*Solid Jewel Tones*)
- white pen: Pentel Milky Gel Roller
- red pen: Zig® Writer
- black, green pens: Sakura Gelly Roll

fingers

*This paper is also available by the sheet.

Frog with Tree Branch

- patterned Paper Pizazz™: green screen (*Mixing Jewel Patterned Papers*); barnwood* (*Country*)
- solid Paper Pizazz™: white (*Plain Pastels*); black, green (*Solid Jewel Tones*)
- black pen: Sakura Gelly Roll

left fingers

right fingers

Frolicking Flower Blossoms

- patterned Paper Pizazz™: yellow checks, blue checks, pink checks (*Bright Tints*)
- solid Paper Pizazz™: white (*Plain Pastels*); black (*Solid Jewel Tones*)
- yellow, blue, pink decorating chalks: Craf-T Products
- black pen: Sakura Gelly Roll

*This paper is also available by the sheet.

Garden Gloves

- patterned Paper Pizazz™: green check*, green with dots* (*Hunter Green Coordinating Colors*™)
- solid Paper Pizazz™: pink, yellow (*Plain Pastels*); black (*Solid Jewel Tones*)
- white decorating chalk: Craf-T Products
- white pen: Pentel Milky Gel Roller
- black pen: Sakura Gelly Roll

green checks* (*Paper Pizazz™ Green & White Coordinating Colors™*); vellum pansies (*Paper Pizazz™ Floral Vellum Papers*); forest green (*Paper Pizazz™ Solid Jewel Tones*)

*This paper is also available by the sheet.

Ghost #1

- patterned Paper Pizazz™: white moiré (by the sheet)
- solid Paper Pizazz™: black (*Solid Jewel Tones*)
- red decorating chalk: Craf-T Products
- black, red pens: Zig® Millennium

Ghost #2

- specialty Paper Pizazz™: vellum swirls* (*Vellum Papers*)
- red decorating chalk: Craf-T Products
- black, red pens: Zig® Millennium

Ghost #3

- patterned Paper Pizazz™: white satin (by the sheet)
- solid Paper Pizazz™: black (*Solid Jewel Tones*)
- red decorating chalk: Craf-T Products
- black, red pens: Zig® Millennium

88

*This paper is also available by the sheet.

Ghost #4

- specialty Paper Pizazz™: vellum dots* (*Vellum Papers*)
- red decorating chalk: Craf-T Products
- black, red pens: Zig® Millennium

Ghost with Pumpkin

- specialty Paper Pizazz™: vellum swirls* (*Vellum Papers*)
- solid Paper Pizazz™: orange (*Plain Brights*); black, green (*Solid Jewel Tones*)
- blue decorating chalk: Craf-T Products
- white pen: Pentel Milky Gel Roller
- black pen: Zig® Writer

nose

This paper is also available by the sheet.

Giraffe Pull Toy

- patterned Paper Pizazz™: yellow dots, pink gingham (*Soft Tints*); barnwood* (*Country*)
- solid Paper Pizazz™: brown, tan (*Solid Muted Tones*); white (*Plain Pastels*)
- pink decorating chalk: Craf-T Products
- white pen: Pentel Milky Gel Roller
- black, dark pink pens: Zig® Millennium

spots

cut 2

cut 2

cut 2

● A ¼" wide hole punch and a ¼" wide heart punch make perfect patterns.

neck spots

*This paper is also available by the sheet.

pink gingham, pink check, pink stripe, yellow/ivory stripe, yellow/ivory gingham, yellow squiggle lines (*Paper Pizazz™ Soft Tints*); pink, white, ivory (*Paper Pizazz™ Plain Pastels*)

Girl Brushing Teeth

- patterned Paper Pizazz™: teal/purple plaid, fuchsia roses, teal sprigs, teal/purple stripes (*Mixing Jewel Patterned Papers*); potato chips (*Yummy Papers*); speckled white (*Bj's Handpainted Papers*)
- specialty Paper Pizazz™: silver* (by the sheet)
- solid Paper Pizazz™: white, ivory (*Plain Pastels*); black (*Solid Jewel Tones*)
- peach, pink, orange-red gray decorating chalks: Craf-T Products
- white pen: Pentel Milky Gel Roller
- black, red pens: Zig® Writer

back hand

front hand

toothbrush handle

foot

back slipper

← *cut 2*

*This paper is also available by the sheet.

Girl in Bathtub

- patterned Paper Pizazz™: yarn, gold brushed (*Textured Papers*); barnwood* (*Country*); cream speckled (*Bj's Handpainted Papers*); bubbles* (*Baby*); peach with white flowers, green fleur de lis, purple leaves (*Mixing Soft Patterned Papers*); burgundy with wheat (*Mixing Jewel Patterned Papers*)
- solid Paper Pizazz™: white, ivory (*Plain Pastels*); black (*Solid Jewel Tones*)
- gold, orange, yellow-orange, orange-red, peach, pink, white decorating chalks: Craf-T Products
- white pen: Pentel Milky Gel Roller
- black, red pens: Zig® Writer

right hand fingers

left fingers

bristle side

nose

paw

cut two

cat tail

bristle base

book pages

book cover

left tub leg

SOAP

right tub leg

bubble

*This paper is also available by the sheet.

Give Thanks

- patterned Paper Pizazz™: handpainted with gold leaves border (*Bj's Gold & Handpainted Papers*); fall leaves (by the sheet); gold/brown/rust plaid* (*Jewel Plaids*); barnwood* (*Country*)
- solid Paper Pizazz™: black (*Solid Jewel Tones*)
- orange-red, orange, gold, rust decorating chalks: Craf-T Products
- black pen: Zig® Writer

back of leaf

front of leaf

*This paper is also available by the sheet.

93

Golden Hound Dog

- patterned Paper Pizazz™: gold sponged stars* (*A Woman's Scrapbook*); brown plaid* (*Great Outdoors*); crushed suede* (*Black & White Photos*)
- solid Paper Pizazz™: dark pink, white (*Plain Pastels*); brown (*Solid Muted Colors*); black (*Solid Jewel Tones*)
- white pen: Pentel Milky Gel Roller
- black pen: Zig® Millennium

tongue

nose

eyes

cut 2

white eyes

eye lids

Graduate

- patterned Paper Pizazz™: navy suede* (*Heritage Papers*); gold sponged stars* (*A Woman's Scrapbook*)
- solid Paper Pizazz™: red (*Plain Brights*); light yellow, ivory (*Plain Pastels*); brown (*Solid Muted Colors*); black (*Solid Jewel Tones*)
- pink, peach white decorating chalks: Craf-T Products
- black, red pens: Zig® Writer

tassle

shoes

hair

right hand

left hand

*This paper is also available by the sheet.

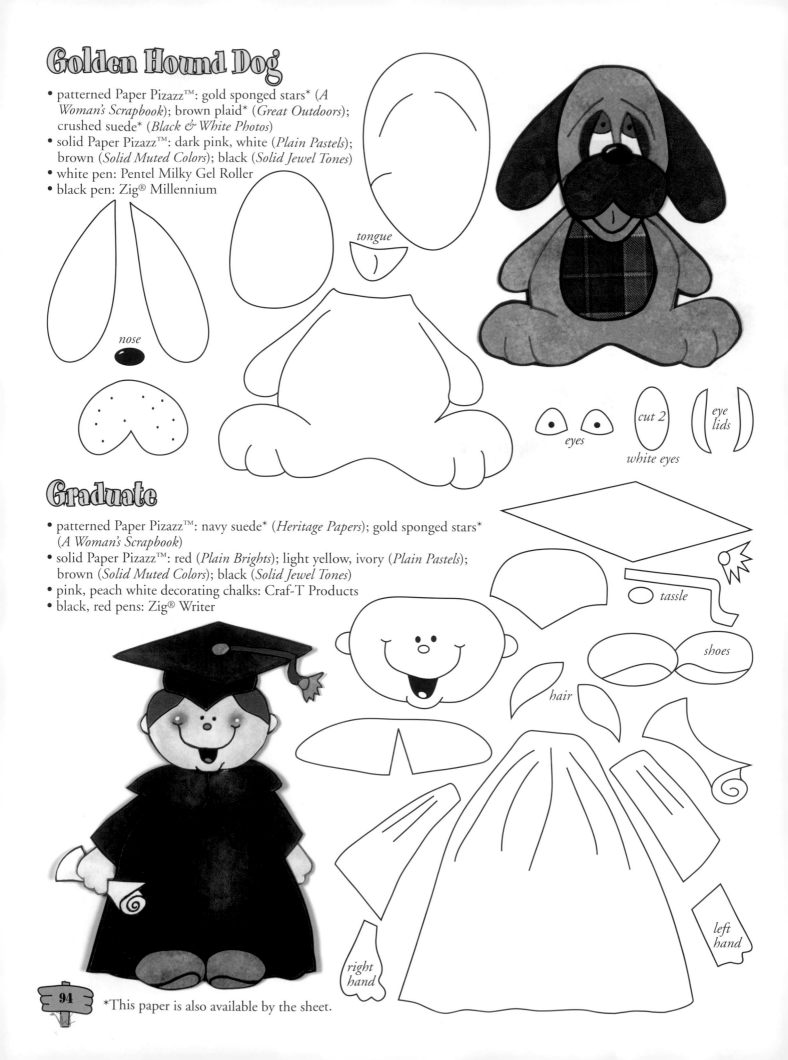

Halloween Tree

- patterned Paper Pizazz™: barnwood* (*Country*)
- solid Paper Pizazz™: yellow (*Plain Brights*); black (*Solid Jewel Tones*)
- red, brown decorating chalks: Craf-T Products
- white pen: Pentel Milky Gel Roller
- black, red pens: Zig® Millennium

stary night, grass (*Paper Pizazz™ by the sheet*); orange/black check (*Paper Pizazz™ Orange & Black Coordinating Colors™*); silver pen (*Pentel Metallic Silver Gel Roller*)

*This paper is also available by the sheet.

Happy Easter

- patterned Paper Pizazz™: blue swirls, pink swirls, yellow swirls, yellow gingham, pink gingham, green gingham, green stripe, yellow dots, yellow checks, blue grid (*Bright Tints*)
- solid Paper Pizazz™: black (*Solid Jewel Tones*)
- green glitter pen: Sakura Gelly Roll
- pink pen: Pentel Milky Gel Roller
- black, orange, yellow pens: Zig® Writer

top pink gingham egg

green gingham stripes

top pink gingham egg

left ribbon back

yellow/green egg bottom

cut 1 blue grid, 1 pink gingham

cut 1 pink swirls, 1 yellow gingham

left end of ribbon

left egg stripes

pink gingham bottom

❣ *Color in the grid pattern with the green and yellow pens.*

Happy Holidays

- patterned Paper Pizazz™: gold sponged stars*, green sponged, blue sponged (*A Woman's Scrapbook*); white moiré (by the sheet); red moiré* (*Black & White Photos*)
- solid Paper Pizazz™: black (*Solid Jewel Tones*)
- red, pink decorating chalks: Craf-T Products
- red metallic pen: Marvy® Uchida Gel Sparkles
- white pen: Pentel Milky Gel Roller
- black, metallic green: Sakura Gelly Roll

*This paper is also available by the sheet.

Hearts Smiling

- patterned Paper Pizazz™: red moiré* (*Black & White Photos*); pink moiré*, pink lace (by the sheet); black satin (*Heritage Papers*)
- solid Paper Pizazz™: black (*Solid Jewel Tones*)
- red, white decorating chalks: Craf-T Products
- pink pen: Pentel Milky Gel Roller
- black pen: Zig® Writer

hat

hat brim

white dot on black* (*Paper Pizazz™ Black & White Coordinating Colors™*); red moiré* (*Paper Pizazz™ Black & White Photos*); laser lace* (*Paper Pizazz™ Romantic Papers*)

*This paper is also available by the sheet.

Holly Cluster

- patterned Paper Pizazz™: green with white dots (*Red & Green Coordinating Colors*™)
- solid Paper Pizazz™: red (*Red & Green Coordinating Colors*™); black (*Solid Jewel Tones*)
- white pen: Pentel Milky Gel Roller
- black pen: Sakura Gelly Roll

Holly Leaves

- patterned Paper Pizazz™: green with white dots (*Red & Green Coordinating Colors*™)
- solid Paper Pizazz™: red (*Red & Green Coordinating Colors*™); black (*Solid Jewel Tones*)
- white pen: Pentel Milky Gel Roller
- black pen: Sakura Gelly Roll

Jack-o-Lantern #1

- patterned Paper Pizazz™: orange with white dots (*Orange & Black Coordinating Colors*™)
- solid Paper Pizazz™: green, brown (*Solid Muted Colors*); red (*Plain Brights*); white (*Plain Pastels*); black (*Solid Jewel Tones*)
- red, brown decorating chalks: Craf-T Products
- black pen: Zig® Millennium

○ *cut 2*

● *A ¼" wide hole punch makes perfect circles.*

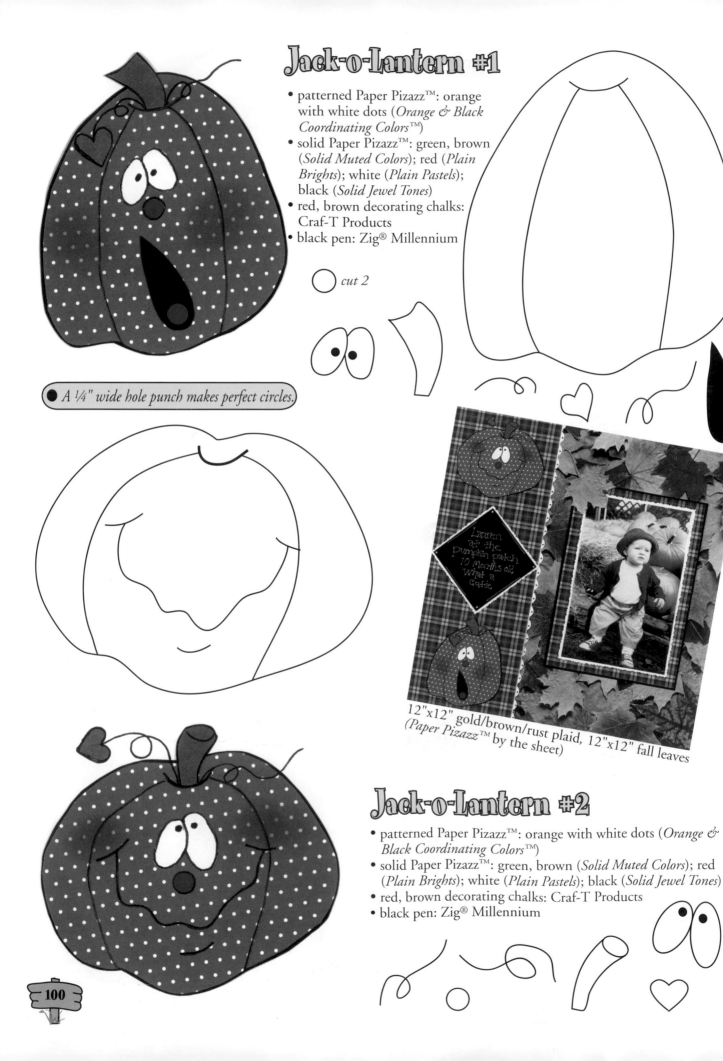

12"x12" gold/brown/rust plaid, 12"x12" fall leaves (*Paper Pizazz*™ by the sheet)

Jack-o-Lantern #2

- patterned Paper Pizazz™: orange with white dots (*Orange & Black Coordinating Colors*™)
- solid Paper Pizazz™: green, brown (*Solid Muted Colors*); red (*Plain Brights*); white (*Plain Pastels*); black (*Solid Jewel Tones*)
- red, brown decorating chalks: Craf-T Products
- black pen: Zig® Millennium

Jack-o-Lantern with Bat

- patterned Paper Pizazz™: purple with orange hollow dots (*A Girl's Scrapbook*)
- solid Paper Pizazz™: orange, black (*Solid Jewel Tones*)
- gold, orange, orange-red decorating chalks: Craf-T Products
- white, pink pens: Pentel Milky Gel Roller
- black, red pens: Zig® Writer

nose

paws

Jack-o-Lantern Pair

- patterned Paper Pizazz™: orange/black gingham* (*Orange & Black 12"x12" Coordinating Colors*™)
- solid Paper Pizazz™: yellow (*Plain Brights*); black, brown, green (*Solid Jewel Tones*)
- orange decorating chalk: Craf-T Products
- yellow pen: Pentel Milky Gel Roller
- black pen: Sakura Gelly Roll

*This paper is also available by the sheet.

Just Say Boo!

- patterned Paper Pizazz™: purple scales (*Mixing Jewel Patterned Papers*); burgundy checks (*Collage Papers*)
- specialty Paper Pizazz™: lace with hollow dots vellum (*Lacy Vellum*)
- solid Paper Pizazz™: white (*Plain Pastels*); black (*Solid Jewel Tones*)
- blue, orange-red, white decorating chalks: Craf-T Products
- white, pink pens: Pentel Milky Gel Roller
- red metallic pen: Marvy® Uchida Gel Sparkler
- black pen: Sakura Gelly Roll

left fingers

← *cut*

❧ *No Halloween photo album would be complete without this banner paper piece pattern!*

Ladybug Flying with Daisy

- patterned Paper Pizazz™: white dot on red* (*Ho, Ho, Ho!!!*); forest green suede* (*Making Heritage Scrapbook Pages*)
- solid Paper Pizazz™: white (*Plain Pastels*); yellow (*Plain Brights*); black (*Solid Jewel Tones*)
- red, white decorating chalks: Craf-T Products
- white pen: Pentel Milky Gel Roller
- black, red pens: Zig® Millennium

right fingers

cape patches

arm

back cape

left hand

front cape

flower center

Ladybug in Glove

- patterned Paper Pizazz™: red/black checks* (*Bold & Bright*); yellow dots (*Soft Tints*); forest green suede* (*Making Heritage Scrapbook Pages*)
- solid Paper Pizazz™: ivory, white (*Plain Pastels*); brown, black (*Solid Jewel Tones*)
- red decorating chalk: Craf-T Products
- white pen: Pentel Milky Gel Roller
- black, red pens: Zig® Millennium

left hand

right hand

head

inside top of glove

bow tail

bow tail

cut 2

bow folds

bow tail

*This paper is also available by the sheet.

Ladybug Sitting on Daisy

- patterned Paper Pizazz™: red with hollow dots* (*Bold & Bright*); forest green suede* (*Making Heritage Scrapbook Pages*)
- solid Paper Pizazz™: yellow (*Plain Brights*); white (*Plain Pastels*); black (*Solid Jewel Tones*)
- white, brown, red decorating chalks: Craf-T Products
- white pen: Pentel Milky Gel Roller
- black, red pens: Zig® Millennium

right hand

right leaf

left hand

left leaf

ZAKKARY is... Cute AS A BUG

ladybugs* (*Paper Pizazz*™ by the sheet); black with white dots (*Paper Pizazz*™ *Black & White Coordinating Colors*™); white (*Paper Pizazz*™ *Plain Pastels*); black (*Paper Pizazz*™ *Solid Jewel Tones*)

*This paper is also available by the sheet.

Ladybug in Watering Can

- patterned Paper Pizazz™: yellow/black check*, red/black vertical stripe* (*Bold & Bright*)
- solid Paper Pizazz™: red (*Plain Brights*); white, light yellow (*Plain Pastels*); black (*Solid Jewel Tones*)
- red decorating chalk: Craf-T Products
- white pen: Pentel Milky Gel Roller
- black, yellow, red pens: Zig® Millennium

inside top of can

cut 2

right hand

left hand

wheel

cut 2

Ladybug Waving

- patterned Paper Pizazz™: red/black checks* (*Bold & Bright*)
- solid Paper Pizazz™: white (*Plain Pastels*); black (*Solid Jewel Tones*)
- red, white decorating chalks: Craf-T Products
- white pen: Pentel Milky Gel Roller
- black, red pens: Zig® Millennium

*This paper is also available by the sheet.

Ladybug with Watermelon Slice

- patterned Paper Pizazz™: pink swirls, green gingham (*Bright Tints*); handmade black, handmade ivory (*"Handmade" Papers*)
- solid Paper Pizazz™: black (*Solid Jewel Tones*)
- pink, orange-red decorating chalks: Craf-T Products
- white pen: Pentel Milky Gel Roller
- black, red pens: Zig® Writer

left fingers

right fingers

right foot

left foot

seed
cut 3

blue stars (*Paper Pizazz™ by the sheet*); pink swirls, pink grid (*Paper Pizazz™ Bright Tints*); white, blue (*Paper Pizazz™ Plain Pastels*); black (*Paper Pizazz™ Solid Jewel Tones*); alphabet template (*Fat Caps, Francis Meyer®*)

106

Lambs

- patterned Paper Pizazz™: lavender swirls, pink swirls, green swirls (*Soft Tints*)
- solid Paper Pizazz™: lavender, dark pink, green (*Plain Pastels*); black (*Solid Jewel Tones*)
- red decorating chalk: Craf-T Products
- white pen: Pentel Milky Gel Roller
- black pen: Zig® Millennium

tail

cut 3

ears

cut 3 pairs

cut 2

cut 2

cut 2

back legs

cut 3 pairs

front legs

Lion

- patterned Paper Pizazz™: crushed suede* (*Black & White Photos*); gold sponged stars* (*A Woman's Scrapbook*)
- solid Paper Pizazz™: black (*Solid Jewel Tones*)
- red decorating chalk: Craf-T Products
- white pen: Pentel Milky Gel Roller
- black pen: Zig® Millennium

outer ear

cut 2

inner ear

cut 2

left paw

inner mane

nose

outer mane

right paw

*This paper is also available by the sheet.

Moon

- patterned Paper Pizazz™: gold sponged stars* (*A Woman's Scrapbook*)
- solid Paper Pizazz™: black (*Solid Jewel Tones*)
- white, pink decorating chalks: Craf-T Products
- white pen: Pentel Milky Gel Roller
- black pen: Sakura Gelly Roll

● *A ⅛" wide hole punch makes perfect circles.*

Moon, Cloud & Stars

- patterned Paper Pizazz™: clouds* (*Vacation*)
- solid Paper Pizazz™: yellow (*Solid Muted Colors*); black (*Solid Jewel Tones*)
- brown, tan, gold, white decorating chalks: Craf-T Products
- black, red pens: Zig® Writer

cut 3

❣ *To create a 3-D look attach a small piece of foam mounting tape behind each star.*

*This paper is also available by the sheet.

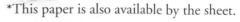

Moon with Star

- patterned Paper Pizazz™: blue dots (*Soft Tints*); yellow dots (*Bright Tints*)
- solid Paper Pizazz™: black (*Solid Jewel Tones*)
- red decorating chalk: Craf-T Products
- white pen: Pentel Milky Gel Roller
- red, black pens: Zig® Millennium

yellow stripes, yellow sqiggle lines, blue diamonds
(*Paper Pizazz™ 12"x12" Soft Tints*)

additional star pattern

Mouse with Cheese

- patterned Paper Pizazz™: red & white stripes* (*Ho, Ho, Ho!!!*); yellow dots (*Soft Tints*)
- solid Paper Pizazz™: red (*Plain Brights*); ivory, dark pink (*Plain Pastels*); gray, black (*Solid Jewel Tones*)
- red, black decorating chalks: Craf-T Products
- white pen: Pentel Milky Gel Roller
- black pen: Zig® Millennium

mouth

nose

inner ears

hand

*This paper is also available by the sheet.

● *A ¼" wide hole punch makes perfect circles.*

Mouse with Stars

- patterned Paper Pizazz™: white with red stripes (*Red & White Coordinating Colors™*); green dots (*Bright Tints*)
- solid Paper Pizazz™: red, yellow (*Plain Brights*); dark pink, ivory, white (*Plain Pastels*); gray, black (*Solid Jewel Tones*)
- red, pink, brown decorating chalks: Craf-T Products
- white pen: Pentel Milky Gel Roller
- red, black pens: Zig® Millennium

inner ears

tail

mouth

hands

left ear

right ear

tail

Mouse Wind-up Toy

- patterned Paper Pizazz™: diagonal ribbons* (*Romantic Papers*); girl power* (*A Girl's Scrapbook*)
- solid Paper Pizazz™: yellow (*Plain Brights*); black (*Solid Jewel Tones*)
- pink decorating chalk: Craf-T Products
- black pen: Sakura Gelly Roll

*This paper is also available by the sheet.

111

Mouse with Watering Can

- patterned Paper Pizazz™: purple leaves, flowers on pink, yellow with green stripes (*Mixing Soft Patterned Papers*)
- solid Paper Pizazz™: tan, green (*Solid Muted Colors*); white, ivory (*Plain Pastels*); black, brown (*Solid Jewel Tones*)
- brown, yellow, pink decorating chalks: Craf-T Products
- white pen: Pentel Milky Gel Roller
- black, purple pens: Sakura Gelly Roll

right hand

left hand

inner ears

sleeve ruffle

sleeve

right leg

left leg

water can stripes

tail

*This paper is also available by the sheet.

purple starbursts (Paper Pizazz™ Great Backgrounds); purple sponged* (Paper Pizazz™ Pretty Papers); 12"x12" vellum field of flowers* (Paper Pizazz™ by the sheet); purple vellum (Paper Pizazz™ Pastel Vellum Papers)

Owl

- patterned Paper Pizazz™: brown tri-dots, brown plaid* (*Brown & White Coordinating Colors*™)
- solid Paper Pizazz™: yellow, tan, green, forest green (*Solid Muted Colors*); white (*Plain Pastels*); black (*Solid Jewel Tones*)
- black pen: Zig® Millennium

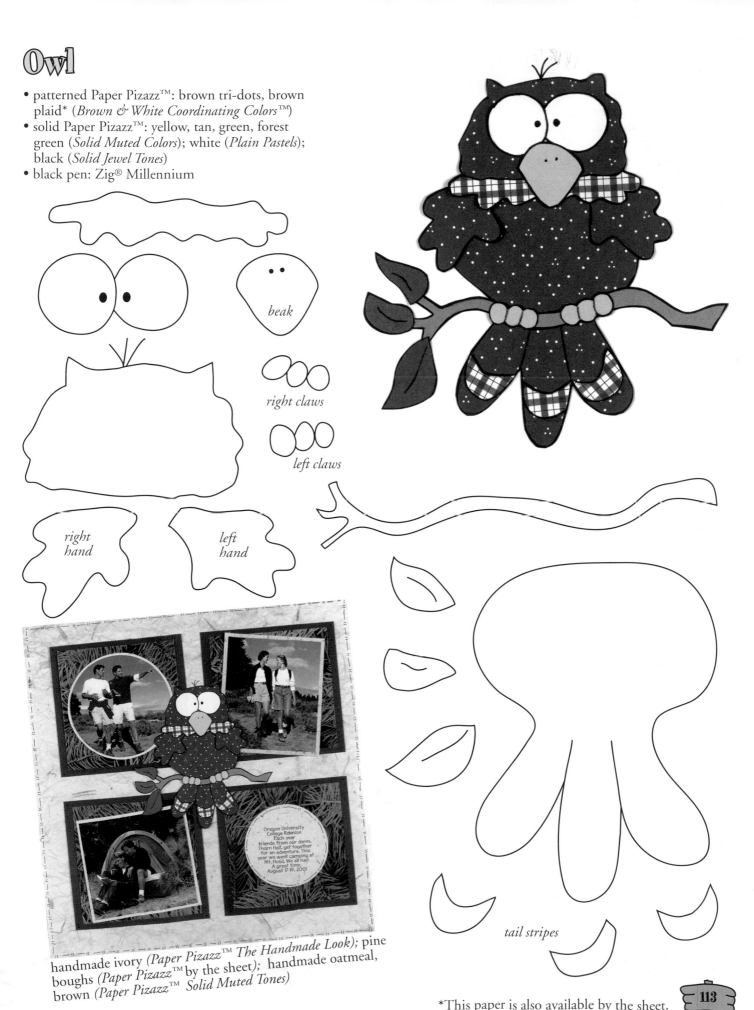

beak

right claws

left claws

right hand

left hand

tail stripes

handmade ivory (*Paper Pizazz*™ *The Handmade Look*); pine boughs (*Paper Pizazz*™ *by the sheet*); handmade oatmeal, brown (*Paper Pizazz*™ *Solid Muted Tones*)

*This paper is also available by the sheet.

Owl with Books

- patterned Paper Pizazz™: blue sponged, green sponged, brown sponged, brown spattered, gold spattered (*Spattered, Crackled, Sponged*); cork board* (*School Days*); gold brush strokes (*Textured Papers*); red moiré* (*Black & White Photos*)
- solid Paper Pizazz™: black (*Solid Jewel Tones*)
- white, black, red decorating chalks: Craf-T Products
- white pen: Pentel Milky Gel Roller
- black pen: Zig® Writer

beak

top book bands

bottom book bands

frame

bottom book

top book

School's
OUT!

tan diamonds (*Paper Pizazz™ Mixing Jewel Patterned Papers*); blue sponged* (*Paper Pizazz™ Spattered, Crackled & Sponged*); brown, blue (*Paper Pizazz™ Solid Muted Colors*)

*This paper is also available by the sheet.

Owl with Diploma

- patterned Paper Pizazz™: crushed suede* (*Black & White Photos*)
- solid Paper Pizazz™: yellow (*Solid Muted Colors*); white (*Plain Pastels*); black (*Solid Jewel Tones*)
- white pen: Pentel Milky Gel Roller
- black pen: Zig® Millennium

beak

right wing

left wing

left claws

right claws

right tail

center tail

left tail

*This paper is also available by the sheet.

115

Pacifier

- patterned Paper Pizazz™: green gingham, blue dots, pink swirls (*Bright Tints*)
- solid Paper Pizazz™: black (*Solid Jewel Tones*)
- black pen: Zig® Writer

bow knot

yellow gingham, pink gingham (*Paper Pizazz™ Bright Tints*); dark pink, yellow (*Paper Pizazz™ Plain Brights*); white (*Paper Pizazz™ Plain Pastels*)

Penguin with Ice Cube #1

- patterned Paper Pizazz™: black with white dots* (*Heritage Papers*); white moiré (by the sheet)
- specialty Paper Pizazz™: blue vellum (*Pastel Vellum Papers*)
- solid Paper Pizazz™: goldenrod (*Plain Brights*); black (*Solid Jewel Tones*)
- red decorating chalk: Craf-T Products
- black pen: Sakura Gelly Roll

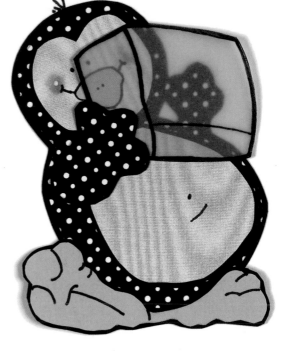

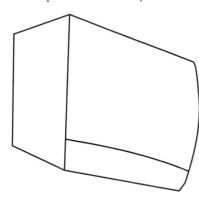

right hand

beak

❦ *You can build a stack of vellum ice cubes and place the penguin on top!*

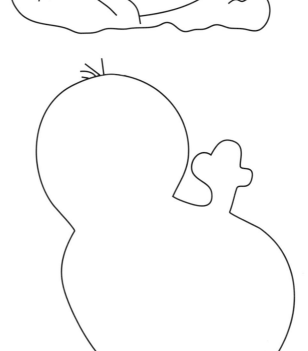

red/black plaid (*Paper Pizazz™ Jewel Plaids*); white (*Paper Pizazz™ Plain Pastels*); black (*Paper Pizazz™ Solid Jewel Tones*)

*This paper is also available by the sheet.

Penguin with Ice Cube #2

- patterned Paper Pizazz™: black with white dots*, green moiré (*Heritage Papers*); white moiré (by the sheet)
- specialty Paper Pizazz™: blue vellum (*Pastel Vellum Papers*)
- solid Paper Pizazz™: goldenrod (*Plain Brights*); black (*Solid Jewel Tones*)
- red decorating chalk: Craf-T Products
- black pen: Sakura Gelly Roll

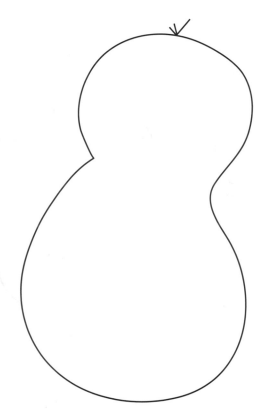

right ear muff

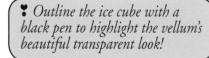
left ear muff

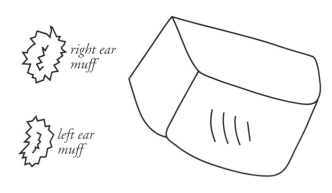

right hand

left fingers

❣ *Outline the ice cube with a black pen to highlight the vellum's beautiful transparent look!*

beak

right foot

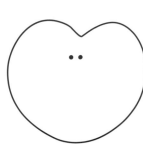
left foot

*This paper is also available by the sheet.

Penguin with Ice Cube #3

- patterned Paper Pizazz™: black with white dots*, red velvet (*Heritage Papers*); white moiré (by the sheet)
- specialty Paper Pizazz™: blue vellum (*Pastel Vellum Papers*)
- solid Paper Pizazz™: goldenrod (*Plain Brights*); black (*Solid Jewel Tones*)
- red decorating chalk: Craf-T Products
- white pen: Pentel Milky Gel Roller
- black pen: Sakura Gelly Roll

beak

Penguin with Peppermint

- patterned Paper Pizazz™: white dot on red* (*Ho, Ho, Ho!!!*); green tri-dots (*Green & White Coordinating Colors*™)
- solid Paper Pizazz™: yellow (*Plain Brights*); white (*Plain Pastels*); black (*Solid Jewel Tones*)
- red decorating chalk: Craf-T Products
- black pen: Zig® Millennium

beak

right foot

left foot

head

hat rim

left hand

right hand

*This paper is also available by the sheet.

Penguin with Star

- patterned Paper Pizazz™: green dots, green stripes (*Bright Tints*); white dot on red* (*Ho, Ho, Ho!!!*)
- solid Paper Pizazz™: yellow (*Plain Brights*); white (*Plain Pastels*); black (*Solid Jewel Tones*)
- red decorating chalk: Craf-T Products
- black pen: Zig® Millennium

beak

right foot

head

Penguin with Tree Ornament

- patterned Paper Pizazz™: white dot on red* (*Ho, Ho, Ho!!!*); green tri-dots (*Green & White Coordinating Colors*™)
- solid Paper Pizazz™: yellow (*Plain Brights*); white (*Plain Pastels*); black, gray (*Solid Jewel Tones*)
- red decorating chalk: Craf-T Products
- black pen: Zig® Millennium

hat trim

beak

head

hand
cut 2

right foot

left foot

● *A ¼" wide hole punch makes perfect circles.*

*This paper is also available by the sheet.

Pie

- patterned Paper Pizazz™: handmade tan, handmade brown (*"Handmade" Papers*); blue moiré (*Light Great Backgrounds*); burlap* (*Country*); red moiré* (*Black & White Photos*)
- solid Paper Pizazz™: yellow (*Solid Muted Colors*); black (*Solid Jewel Tones*)
- white, brown, blue decorating chalks: Craf-T Products
- green pen: Zig® Writer
- black pen: Sakura Gelly Roll

vent holes

leaf

eaten apple peel

full apple stem

cut apple stem

eaten apple stem

lower apple peel

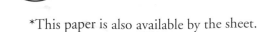

*This paper is also available by the sheet.

Pumpkin

- patterned Paper Pizazz™: gold/brown/rust plaid* (*Jewel Plaids*); grass (by the sheet)
- solid Paper Pizazz™: black, brown (*Solid Jewel Tones*)
- black pen: Sakura Gelly Roll

Rolling Pin with Hot Pads

- patterned Paper Pizazz™: lone star quilt*, Irish chain quilt*, barnwood* (*Country*)
- solid Paper Pizazz™: pink, blue, green (*Solid Muted Tones*); black (*Solid Jewel Tones*)
- black pen: Sakura Gelly Roll

cut 2

cut 2

❣ *Use the center of the star quilt for one of the hot pads and the white square area for the inset pad. Outline the square quilt patches with the black pen to bring dimension to the other hot pad.*

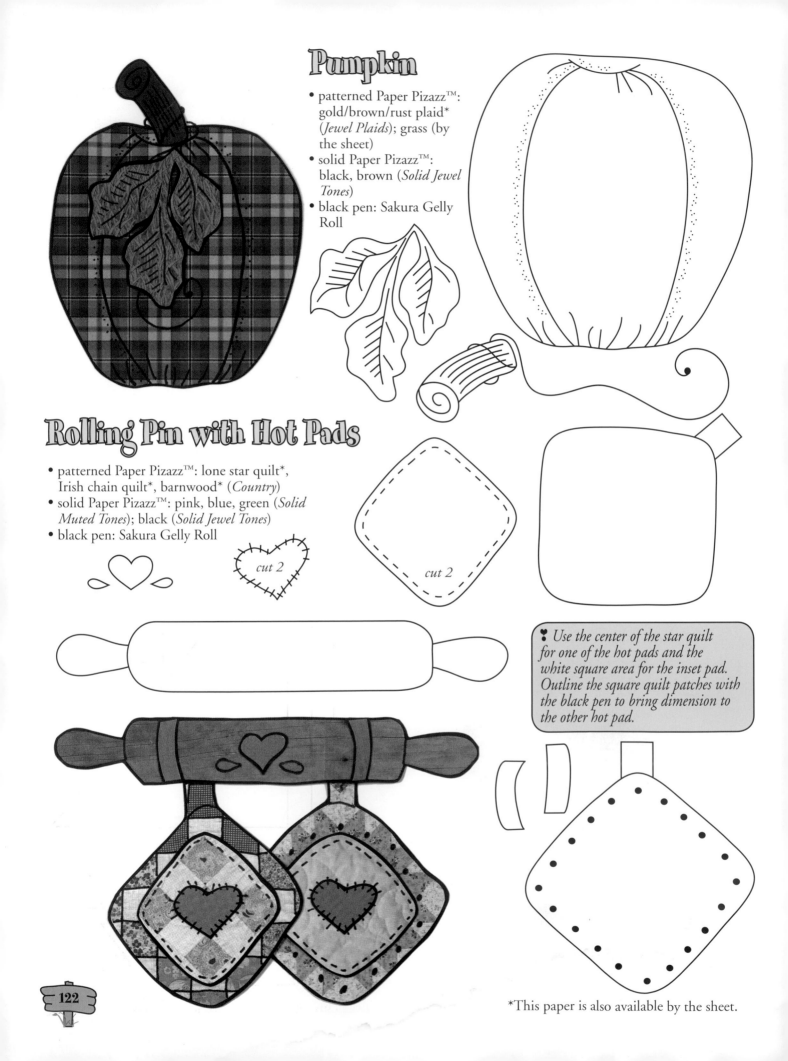

*This paper is also available by the sheet.

Sailboat

- patterned Paper Pizazz™: barnwood* (*Country*); yellow & white checks, yellow with flowers, blue stars, blue & white stripes (*Lisa Williams Blue, Yellow & Green*)
- solid Paper Pizazz™: white, yellow, dark pink (*Plain Pastels*); black (*Solid Jewel Tones*)
- black pen: Zig® Millennium

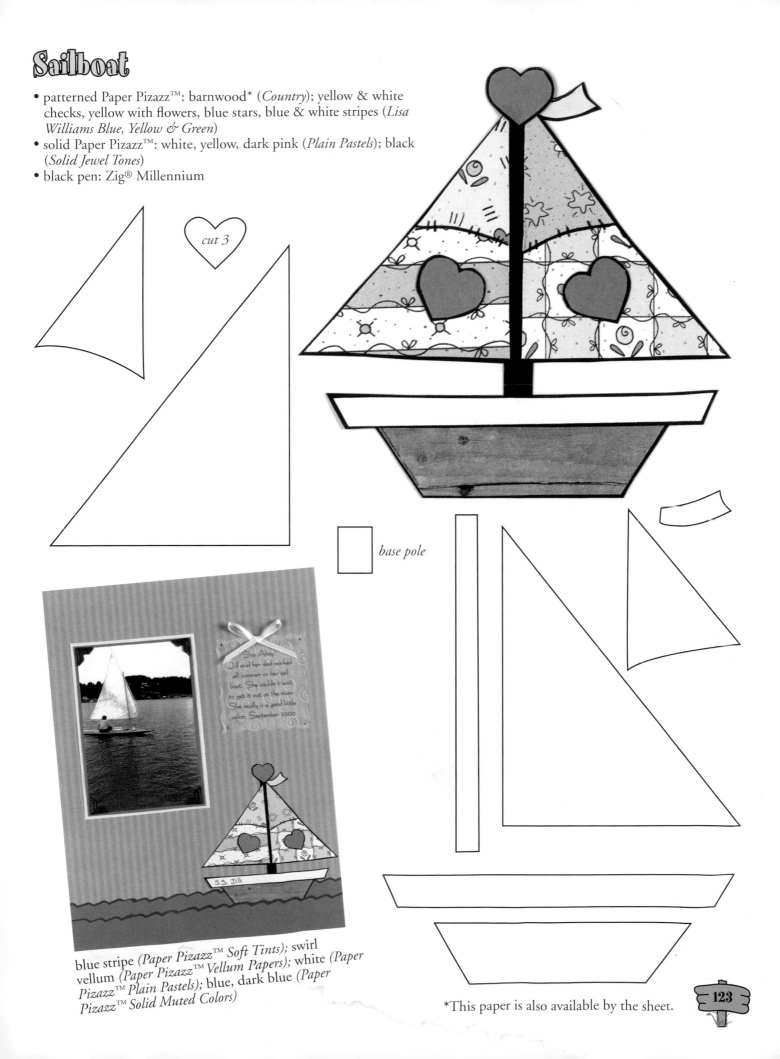

cut 3

base pole

blue stripe (Paper Pizazz™ Soft Tints); swirl vellum (Paper Pizazz™ Vellum Papers); white (Paper Pizazz™ Plain Pastels); blue, dark blue (Paper Pizazz™ Solid Muted Colors)

*This paper is also available by the sheet.

123

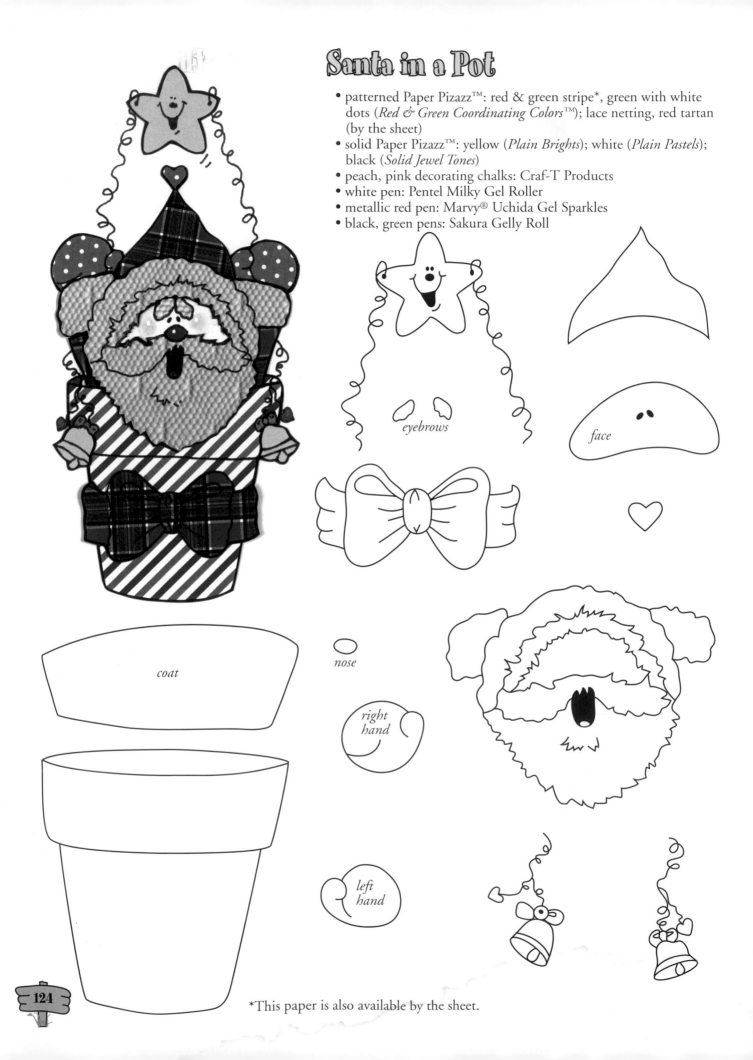

Santa in a Pot

- patterned Paper Pizazz™: red & green stripe*, green with white dots (*Red & Green Coordinating Colors*™); lace netting, red tartan (by the sheet)
- solid Paper Pizazz™: yellow (*Plain Brights*); white (*Plain Pastels*); black (*Solid Jewel Tones*)
- peach, pink decorating chalks: Craf-T Products
- white pen: Pentel Milky Gel Roller
- metallic red pen: Marvy® Uchida Gel Sparkles
- black, green pens: Sakura Gelly Roll

eyebrows

face

coat

nose

right hand

left hand

*This paper is also available by the sheet.

Santa Jack-in-the-Box

- patterned Paper Pizazz™: red & green dots* (*Ho, Ho, Ho!!!*); white moiré (by the sheet); red tartan (by the sheet)
- solid Paper Pizazz™: red, yellow, blue (*Plain Brights*); ivory (*Plain Pastels*); black (*Solid Jewel Tones*)
- peach, pink decorating chalks: Craf-T Products
- white pen: Pentel Milky Gel Roller
- black pen: Sakura Gelly Roll

lid insert panel

crank & knobs

right hand

nose

left hand

face

box lid

box top border

eyebrows

left sleeve trim

right sleeve trim

box bottom border

*This paper is also available by the sheet.

125

Santa with "I Believe" Banner

- patterned Paper Pizazz™: red swirls, green gingham, yellow checks (*Bright Tints*); lace netting (by the sheet)
- solid Paper Pizazz™: ivory, pale blue (*Plain Pastels*); black (*Solid Jewel Tones*)
- orange, pink decorating chalks: Craf-T Products
- white pen: Pentel Milky Gel Roller
- black, red pens: Zig® Writer

left sleeve trim

right sleeve trim

nose

I BELIEVE!

I BELIEVE!

eyebrows

face

right hand

left hand

Santa with Noel Garland

- patterned Paper Pizazz™: red with hollow dots* (*Bold & Bright*); Christmas plaid* (*Ho, Ho, Ho!!!*); Christmas candy*, red & green stripe* (*Red & Green Coordinating Colors™*); lace netting (by the sheet)
- solid Paper Pizazz™: yellow (*Plain Brights*); black (*Solid Jewel Tones*)
- peach, pink decorating chalks: Craf-T Products
- 2" length of 20-gauge yellow plastic wire
- white pen: Pentel Milky Gel Roller
- red pen: Zig® Writer
- black, blue pens: Sakura Gelly Roll

wire fold

NOEL

cut 2

eyebrows

nose

face

sleeve trim

left hand

right hand

right coat trim

left coat trim

♥ *Add to the 3-D look by tying pieces of black thread to the yellow wire, then wrapping it around each letter.*

back coat trim

right foot

left leg

right leg

left foot

127

*This paper is also available by the sheet.

Shower Umbrella

- patterned Paper Pizazz™: pink gingham, yellow stripe, yellow dots (*Soft Tints*)
- solid Paper Pizazz™: yellow (*Solid Muted Colors*); black (*Solid Jewel Tones*)
- black pen: Zig® Millennium

cut 3

cut 2

umbrella back

bow folds

Seahorse

- patterned Paper Pizazz™: green swirl* (*Pretty Papers*); purple smudge (*Bright Great Backgrounds*)
- solid Paper Pizazz™: tan, green, dark green (*Solid Muted Colors*); pink (*Plain Brights*); black (*Solid Jewel Tones*)
- pink decorating chalk: Craf-T Products
- black pen: Zig® Writer

● *A ¼" length leaf punch and a ⅜" wide flower punch make the designs easy to create.*

cut 8

cut 3

*This paper is also available by the sheet.

Smile

- patterned Paper Pizazz™: red grid, yellow swirls, green gingham, blue swirls, purple grid, pink swirls (*Bright Tints*)
- solid Paper Pizazz™: black (*Solid Jewel Tones*)
- pink decorating chalk: Craf-T Products
- white pen: Pentel Milky Gel Roller
- black pen: Zig® Writer

blue stripes with green dots (*Paper Pizazz™ A Girl's Scrapbook*); lime green (*Paper Pizazz™ Plain Brights*); black (*Paper Pizazz™ Solid Jewel Tones*)

Snail #1

- patterned Paper Pizazz™: tie-dye*, brushed purple (*Bright Great Backgrounds*)
- solid Paper Pizazz™: black (*Solid Jewel Tones*)
- black pen: Zig® Writer

tail

*This paper is also available by the sheet.

129

Snail #2

- patterned Paper Pizazz™: pink/yellow gingham, pink swirls (*Soft Tints*)
- solid Paper Pizazz™: black (*Solid Jewel Tones*)
- pink decorating chalk: Craf-T Products
- white pen: Pentel Milky Gel Roller
- black pen: Sakura Gelly Roll

Snail #3

- patterned Paper Pizazz™: lavender/pink diamonds, lavender swirls (*Soft Tints*)
- solid Paper Pizazz™: black (*Solid Jewel Tones*)
- purple decorating chalk: Craf-T Products
- white pen: Pentel Milky Gel Roller
- red pen: Zig® Millennium
- black pen: Sakura Gelly Roll

❣ *Snails are the perfect compliment to your photos of the garden or new lawn renovations.*

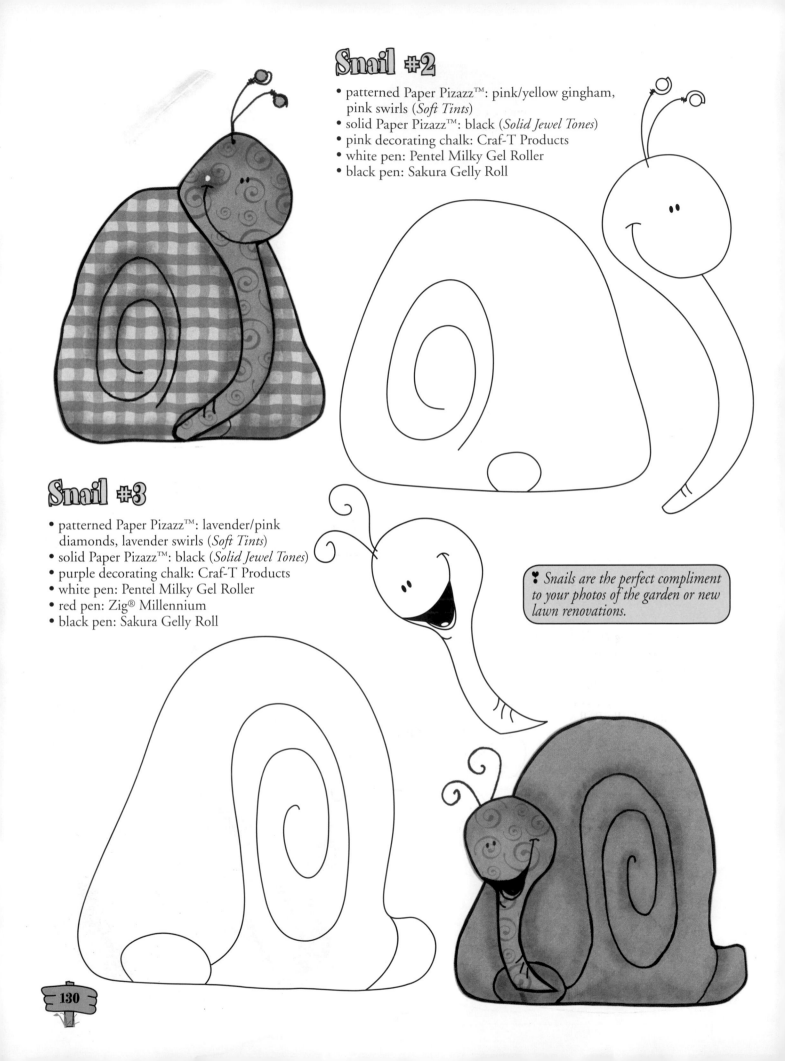

Snail in Bucket

- patterned Paper Pizazz™: green stripes, purple swirls, purple grid (*Bright Tints*); lavender chevrons, lavender tri-dots (*Soft Tints*)
- solid Paper Pizazz™: yellow (*Plain Pastels*); gray, black (*Solid Jewel Tones*)
- purple decorating chalk: Craf-T Products
- white pen: Pentel Milky Gel Rolle
- black pen: Sakura Gelly Roll

left handle

right handle

Snail with Hat

- patterned Paper Pizazz™: purple scales, fuschia rose, tan diamonds (*Mixing Jewel Patterned Papers*)
- solid Paper Pizazz™: lavender, yellow (*Plain Pastels*); black (*Solid Jewel Tones*)
- orange, pink decorating chalks: Craf-T Products
- white pen: Pentel Milky Gel Roller
- black pen: Sakura Gelly Roll

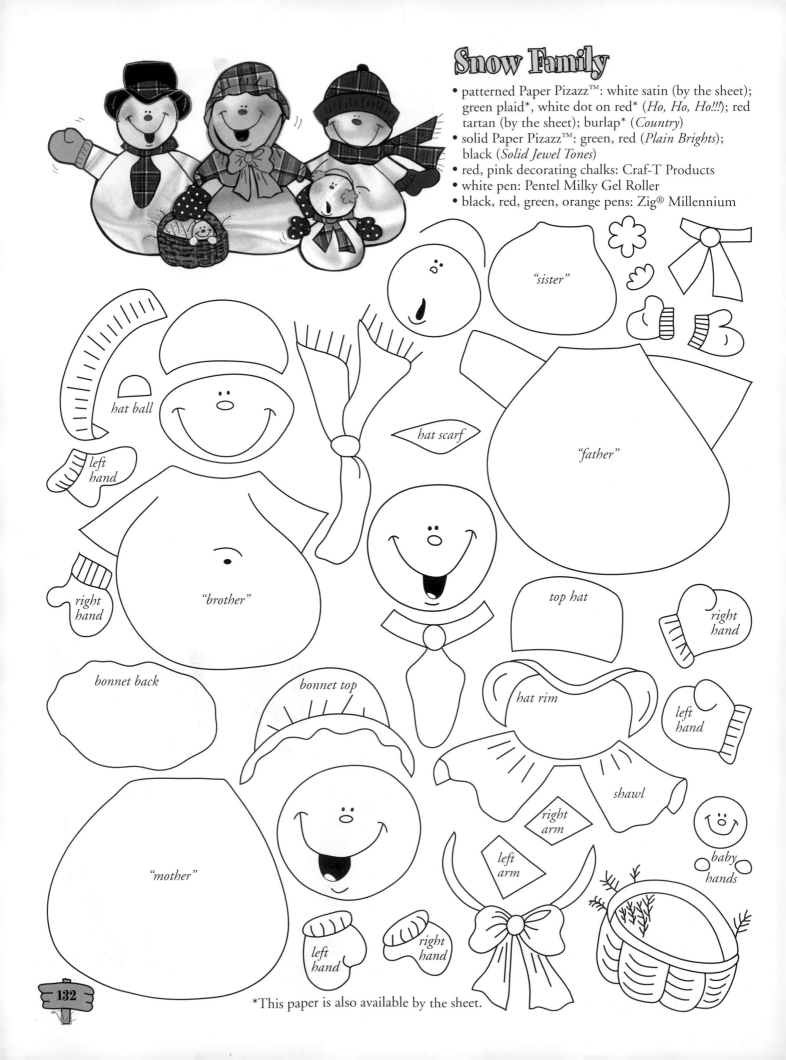

Snow Family

- patterned Paper Pizazz™: white satin (by the sheet); green plaid*, white dot on red* (*Ho, Ho, Ho!!!*); red tartan (by the sheet); burlap* (*Country*)
- solid Paper Pizazz™: green, red (*Plain Brights*); black (*Solid Jewel Tones*)
- red, pink decorating chalks: Craf-T Products
- white pen: Pentel Milky Gel Roller
- black, red, green, orange pens: Zig® Millennium

"sister"

hat ball

left hand

hat scarf

"father"

right hand

"brother"

top hat

right hand

bonnet back

bonnet top

hat rim

left hand

shawl

"mother"

right arm

left arm

baby hands

left hand

right hand

*This paper is also available by the sheet.

Snow Person #1

- patterned Paper Pizazz™: white satin (by the sheet); white dot on red*, red & white stripe* (*Ho, Ho, Ho!!!*); black with white dots* (*Black & White Coordinating Colors™*)
- solid Paper Pizazz™: red (*Plain Brights*); black (*Solid Jewel Tones*)
- pink, red decorating chalks: Craf-T Products
- white pen: Pentel Milky Gel Roller
- black, red pens: Zig® Millennium

left hand

right hand

hat rim

Snow Person #2

- patterned Paper Pizazz™: white satin (by the sheet); red & white stripe* (*Ho, Ho, Ho!!!*); white dots on green (*Red & Green Coordinating Colors™*)
- solid Paper Pizazz™: red (*Plain Brights*); black (*Solid Jewel Tones*)
- pink, red decorating chalks: Craf-T Products
- white pen: Pentel Milky Gel Roller
- black, red pens: Zig® Millennium

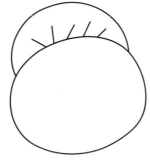

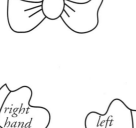

right hand

left hand

snowflakes* (Paper Pizazz™ 12"x12" Christmas Time); white, blue (Paper Pizazz™ Plain Pastels); black (Paper Pizazz™ Solid Jewel Tones); saying (Paper Pizazz™ Tops & Bottoms)

*This paper is also available by the sheet.

Snow Person #3

- patterned Paper Pizazz™: blue corrugated* (*Country*); white satin (by the sheet); red & white stripe* (*Ho, Ho, Ho!!!*)
- solid Paper Pizazz™: red (*Plain Brights*); white (*Plain Pastels*); black (*Solid Jewel Tones*)
- pink, red decorating chalks: Craf-T Products
- white pen: Pentel Milky Gel Roller
- black, red pens: Zig® Millennium

ear muff wire

ear muffs

right hand

left hand

Snow Person #4

- patterned Paper Pizazz™: forest green suede* (*Making Heritage Scrapbook Pages*); white satin (by the sheet); red & white stripe* (*Ho, Ho, Ho!!!*); black with white dots* (*Black & White Coordinating Colors*™)
- solid Paper Pizazz™: black (*Solid Jewel Tones*)
- pink, red decorating chalks: Craf-T Products
- white pen: Pentel Milky Gel Roller
- black, red pens: Zig® Millennium

left arm

right hand

left hand

Snow Person #5

- patterned Paper Pizazz™: blue corrugated* (*Country*); white satin (by the sheet); red & white stripe* (*Ho, Ho, Ho!!!*); white dots on green (*Red & Green Coordinating Colors*™)
- solid Paper Pizazz™: blue (*Plain Brights*); black (*Solid Jewel Tones*)
- pink, red decorating chalks: Craf-T Products
- white pen: Pentel Milky Gel Roller
- black, red pens: Zig® Millennium

right coat

left coat

right sleeve

left sleeve

hat rim

right hand

left hand

*This paper is also available by the sheet.

Snowflake–Small

- patterned Paper Pizazz™: butterflies* (*A Woman's Scrapbook*)
- specialty Paper Pizazz™: vellum blue swirls* (*Colored Vellum Papers*)
- solid Paper Pizazz™: black (*Solid Jewel Tones*)
- blue, white decorating chalks: Craf-T Products
- black, dark pink pens: Zig® Writer

small bottom layer

small snowflake

large center layer

small top layer

large bottom layer

large top layer

large snowflake

Snowflake–Large

- patterned Paper Pizazz™: clouds* (*Vacation*)
- specialty Paper Pizazz™: blue vellum snowflakes* (*Vellum Collection*)
- solid Paper Pizazz™: black (*Solid Jewel Tones*)
- dark blue, blue, white decorating chalks: Craf-T Products
- black, blue pens: Zig® Writer

Sun with Glasses

- patterned Paper Pizazz™: yellow checks, pink checks (*Bright Tints*)
- solid Paper Pizazz™: bright pink (*Plain Brights*); black (*Solid Jewel Tones*)
- pink decorating chalk: Craf-T Products
- black, red pens: Zig® Millennium

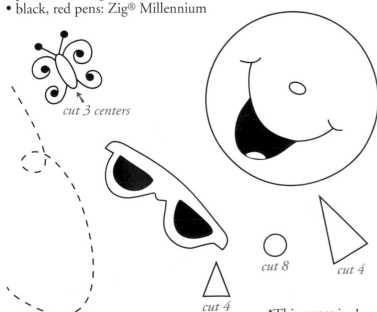

cut 3 centers

cut 8

cut 4

cut 4

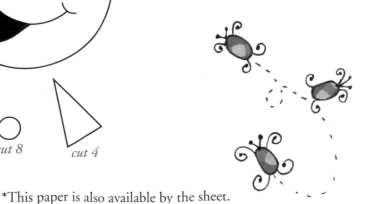

*This paper is also available by the sheet.

Summer Days

- patterned Paper Pizazz™: red/black checks* (*Bold & Bright*); picnic plaid (*The Great Outdoors*); pool water* (*Vacation #2*); sand* (*Textured Papers*); citrus slices (*Yummy Papers*); pink moiré*, lace netting (by the sheet); ladybugs, grass (by the sheet)
- specialty Paper Pizazz™: blue vellum (*Pastel Vellum Papers*)
- solid Paper Pizazz™: white (*Plain Pastels*); red (*Plain Brights*); black (*Solid Jewel Tones*)
- black, orange, red pens: Zig® Writer

flower center

flower center

flower center

sunglasses frame

sunglasses

cut 2

blanket stripe

picnic cloth

snail

blanket back

sea shells

❦ *Make a splash in your scrapbook with this pattern and those summer photos by the pool, beach or picnics in the park.*

*This paper is also available by the sheet.

Summer Vacation

- patterned Paper Pizazz™: pool water* (*Vacation #2*); clouds* (*Vacation*); handmade batik (*The Handmade Look*); grass (by the sheet)
- specialty Paper Pizazz™: green vellum (*Pastel Vellum Papers*); silver* (by the sheet)
- solid Paper Pizazz™: yellow (*Plain Pastels*); black (*Solid Jewel Tones*)
- gold, yellow-orange decorating chalks: Craf-T Products
- mounting adhesive: Therm O Web
- black, red pens: Zig® Writer

cut 2

cut 2

hose

hose

hose

hose

*This paper is also available by the sheet.

Tent with Boy & Puppy

- patterned Paper Pizazz™: blue gingham, yellow gingham, green gingham (*Soft Tints*); grass (by the sheet)
- solid Paper Pizazz™: brown (*Solid Muted Colors*); ivory (*Plain Pastels*); black (*Solid Jewel Tones*)
- peach, pink, red, white decorating chalks: Craf-T Products
- white, pink pens: Pentel Milky Gel Roller
- black, red pens: Zig® Writer

right fingers

left tent

left fingers

left grass

right grass

left flap

right flap

tent inside

right tent

right flap

Toucan

- patterned Paper Pizazz™: colorful stripes* (*Bright Great Backgrounds*)
- solid Paper Pizazz™: yellow, green, red, blue (*Plain Brights*); white (*Plain Pastels*); black (*Solid Jewel Tones*)
- white pen: Pentel Milky Gel Roller
- black pen: Zig® Millennium

beak

right wing

tail feathers

left wing

feet

138

*This paper is also available by the sheet.

Turkey

- patterned Paper Pizazz™: burgundy with wheat, tan diamonds (*Mixing Jewel Patterned Papers*); handmade ivory, handmade brown (*"Handmade" Papers*)
- solid Paper Pizazz™: orange (*Solid Muted Tones*); black (*Solid Jewel Tones*)
- orange decorating chalk: Craf-T Products
- white pen: Pentel Milky Gel Roller
- black pen: Sakura Gelly Roll

tail stripe

tail feathers

right tail stripe

left tail stripe

beak

wattle

left wing stripe

left wing feathers

left wing

right wing

right wing feathers

right wing stripes

♥ *Use this turkey along with a serving of your family Thanksgiving photos.*

Turtle Side View

- patterned Paper Pizazz™: green/blue tortoise shell (*Bright Great Backgrounds*)
- solid Paper Pizazz™: green, blue (*Plain Brights*); black (*Solid Jewel Tones*)
- pink decorating chalk: Craf-T Products
- black pen: Zig® Millennium

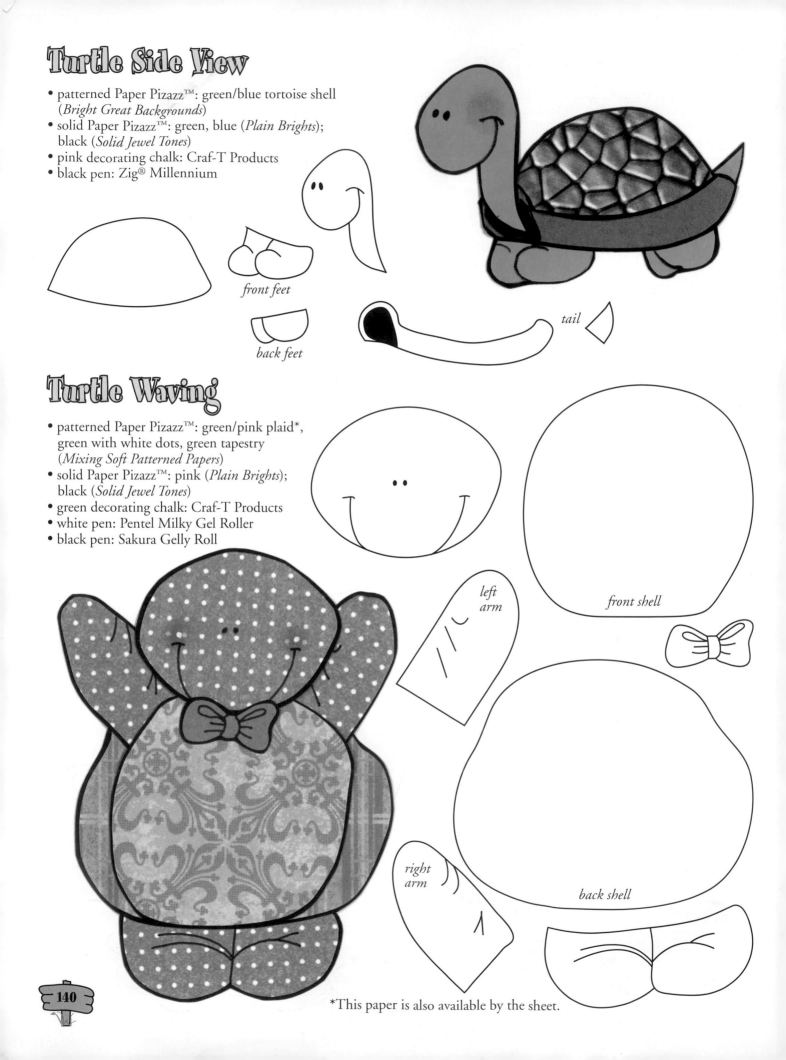

front feet

back feet

tail

Turtle Waving

- patterned Paper Pizazz™: green/pink plaid*, green with white dots, green tapestry (*Mixing Soft Patterned Papers*)
- solid Paper Pizazz™: pink (*Plain Brights*); black (*Solid Jewel Tones*)
- green decorating chalk: Craf-T Products
- white pen: Pentel Milky Gel Roller
- black pen: Sakura Gelly Roll

left arm

front shell

right arm

back shell

*This paper is also available by the sheet.

Turtle with Frog & Bee

- patterned Paper Pizazz™: green/blue tiles (*Bright Great Backgrounds*); yellow dots (*Bright Tints*)
- specialty Paper Pizazz™: lavender vellum (*Pastel Vellum Papers*)
- solid Paper Pizazz™: white (*Plain Pastels*); navy blue, black, dark green (*Solid Jewel Tones*)
- lime green, red decorating chalks: Craf-T Products
- white pen: Pentel Milky Gel Roller
- black pen: Zig® Millennium

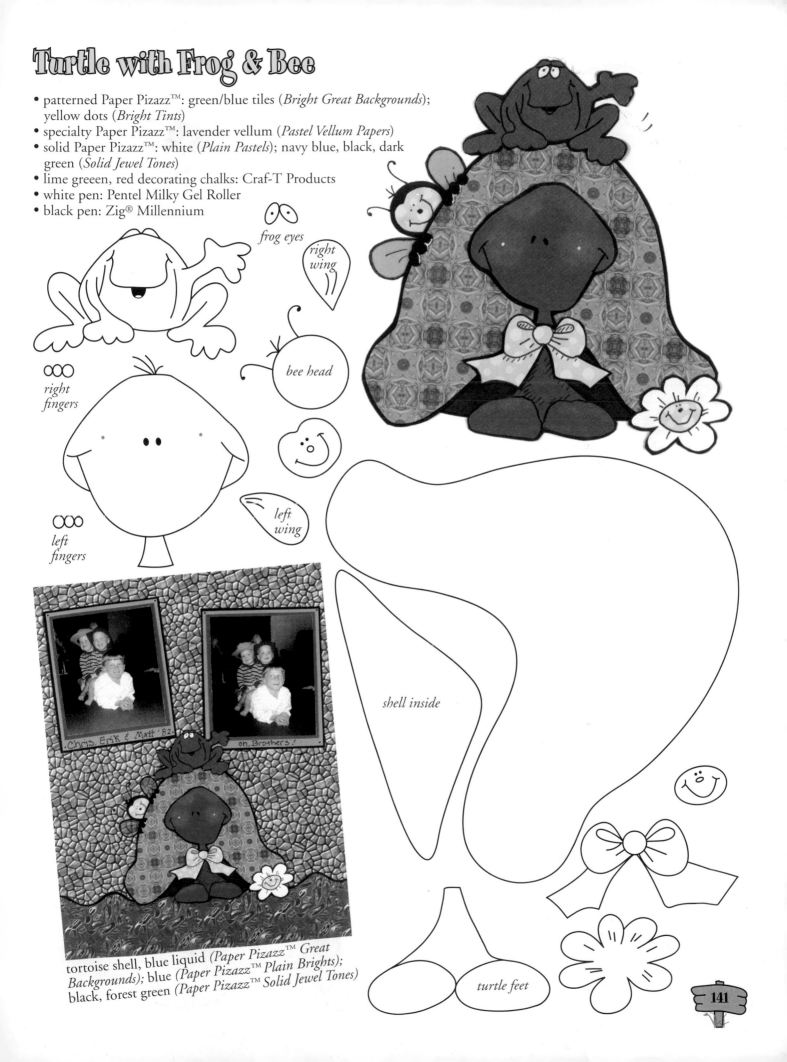

frog eyes

right wing

right fingers

bee head

left wing

left fingers

shell inside

tortoise shell, blue liquid (*Paper Pizazz™ Great Backgrounds*); blue (*Paper Pizazz™ Plain Brights*); black, forest green (*Paper Pizazz™ Solid Jewel Tones*)

turtle feet

Turtle with Life Vest

- patterned Paper Pizazz™: teal swirls (*Mixing Soft Patterned Papers*); teal tiles (*Textured Papers*); red grid (*Bright Tints*)
- solid Paper Pizazz™: yellow, white (*Plain Pastels*); black (*Solid Jewel Tones*)
- blue decorating chalk: Craf-T Products
- black pen: Sakura Gelly Roll

shell

lower shirt

upper shirt

right hand

left hand

Turtle with Pie

- patterned Paper Pizazz™: green diamonds, green gingham, blue stripes, purple stripes (*Bright Tints*)
- solid Paper Pizazz™: tan (*Solid Muted Tones*); white (*Plain Pastels*); black (*Solid Jewel Tones*)
- green, brown decorating chalks: Craf-T Products
- white pen: Pentel Milky Gel Roller
- black pen: Sakura Gelly Roll

doily

Watering Can with Flowers

- patterned Paper Pizazz™: blue corrugated* (*Country*); white flowers (*Floral Papers*)
- solid Paper Pizazz™: light green, pink, yellow (*Plain Pastels*); black, green (*Solid Jewel Tones*)
- blue, black, green decorating chalks: Craf-T Products
- black pen: Sakura Gelly Roll

spout back

blue flower

flower face

cut 3 flower center

watercolor pansies* (Paper Pizazz™ Pretty Papers); vellum ferns (Paper Pizazz™ Vellum Papers); white (Paper Pizazz™ Plain Pastels); black (Paper Pizazz™ Solid Jewel Tones)

Danny & mon 8-3-01

*This paper is also available by the sheet.

Witch

- patterned Paper Pizazz™: green with blue diamonds (*A Girl's Scrapbook*); black with hollow dots (*Bold & Bright*)
- solid Paper Pizazz™: bright green, blue, yellow, pink, red (*Plain Brights*); ivory (*Plain Pastels*); black (*Solid Jewel Tones*)
- blue, pink, peach decorating chalks: Craf-T Products
- white, lavender pens: Pentel Milky Gel Roller
- black pen: Sakura Gelly Roll

lower hair back

hand

nose

bag patch

foot

TRICK TREATS

purple with stars, dots on purple* (Paper Pizazz™ *Purple Coordinating Colors™*)*; blue stars (*Paper Pizazz™ by the sheet*); blue/aqua striped (*Paper Pizazz™ A Girl's Scrapbook*); lime green (*Paper Pizazz™ Plain Brights*); black (*Paper Pizazz™ Solid Jewel Tones*); saying (*Paper Pizazz™ Punch-Outs™ Fall & Halloween*)